"*Prisoners of Hope* will encourage and challenge your spirit as you read the stories of these American heroes. Every one of them served in difficult circumstances, in Vietnam some spent as long as eight years as POWs. Faith and hope brought them through hellish times. I personally heard many of their stories while escorting them on their returning flights out of Hanoi. This book will bring hope to all who read it."
—*Brig Gen Dick Abel, USAF (Ret.), Former Executive Director Military Ministry, Campus Crusade for Christ*

What others are saying about books in the "Gathering of Eagles" series:

"There are no better sources of advice for men of arms than those who have walked the walk in service, meriting the nation's highest honor for valor. Jim Coy is an author who understands the relationship between physical and moral courage and the true source of honor. His own noble standards are part of the greatness of this and his other books."
—*RADM Jeremiah Denton, USN (Ret.), Former U.S. Senator, Ex-POW, Vietnam*

"Any book written by this red, white, and blue Christian author will make a powerful and positive impact on the reader. Everyone who reads it will experience a renewed awareness of what makes America the greatest nation in the world."
—*Brig Gen Robbie Risner, USAF (Ret.), Ace, Korean War, Ex-POW Vietnam*

Prisoners of
HOPE

A Gathering of Eagles, Book Three

Prisoners of
HOPE

A Gathering of Eagles, Book Three

119 Ex-POWs Talk About Leadership, Courage, and Faith

COL Jimmie Dean Coy (Ret.)

E*v*ergreen
PRESS

Other books in the series:

A Gathering of Eagles, Second Edition

VALOR—A Gathering of Eagles

Prisoners of Hope—A Gathering of Eagles Book Three
by COL Jimmie Dean Coy (Ret.)

ISBN: 1-58169-177-7
For Worldwide Distribution
Printed in the U.S.A.

Evergreen Press
P.O. Box 191540 • Mobile, AL 36619
800-367-8203

TABLE OF CONTENTS

Carey Ashcraft, WWII, ETO 2
Kenneth Barney, WWII, ETO 4
William Bearisto, WWII, ETO..8
Paul Bergman, WWII, ETO 10
Robert Bieber, WWII, ETO 12
Donald Boyer, WWII, ETO 16
Vernon Brooks, WWII, ETO...18
William Byrns, Vietnam 20
Robert Carter, WWII, ETO 24
Jon Cavaiani, Vietnam * 26
Robert Certain, Vietnam 28
Fred Cherry, Vietnam...32
Howard Chrisco, WWII, PTO...36
John Clark, Vietnam 38
Jerry Coffee, Vietnam 42
J. Quincy Collins, Vietnam...44
Charles Crandell, USS Pueblo, North Korea.........................46
William Crawford, WWII, ETO* 48
Fred Dallas, WWII, ETO 50
George Day, Vietnam * 52
Irving Day, Jr. WWII, ETO 54
Jeremiah Denton, Vietnam...56
C. Earl Derrington, Jr., WWII, ETO 60
David Eberly, Persian Gulf War 62
Carl Edwards, WWII, ETO 64
Lee Ellis, Vietnam 66
Wendell Fetters, WWII, ETO 68
Stephen Fitzgerald, WWII, ETO 70
William Fornes, Korea 72
William Foster, WWII, ETO...74
Carl Fyler, WWII, ETO..76
Paul Galanti, Vietnam 80
Len Gregg, WWII, ETO 82
Bruce Hall, WWII, ETO 86
Porter Halyburton, Vietnam...88
John Hanson, WWII, PTO 92
Carlyle Harris, Vietnam 94
Gerald Harvey, WWII, ETO..98
Betsy Herold Heimke, WWII, PTO....................................100
Harland Hendrix, WWII, ETO 102
Wayne Hitchcock, WWII, ETO 104

Roger Ingvalson, Vietnam 106
Lloyd Jackson, WWII, PTO 108
Harold Johnson, Vietnam 110
Sam Johnson, Vietnam 112
Kenneth Jones, WWII, ETO 114
George Juskalian, WWII, ETO 116
J. Lawrence King, WWII, ETO 118
John Klumpp, WWII, ETO 120
Frank Kravetz, WWII, ETO 122
Clarence Larson, WWII, PTO 124
Richard Lockhart, WWII, ETO 126
Benedict Lohman, WWII, PTO 128
Cordino Longiotti, WWII, ETO 130
David Ludlum, Korea 132
Leonard Lutjen, WWII, ETO 134
Frank Mace WWII, PTO 136
John Maher, WWII, ETO 138
James McCahon, WWII, PTO 140
John McCain, Vietnam 142
Eugene McDaniel, Vietnam 146
Norman McDaniel, Vietnam 148
J.B. McKamey, Vietnam 152
Willis Meier, WWII, ETO 154
Hiroshi Miyamura, Korea * 156
Paul Montague, Vietnam 158
Mark Moore, WWII, ETO 162
Herschel Morgan, Vietnam 166
William Mottern, WWII, ETO 168
Timon Mouser, WWII, ETO 170
James Mulligan, Vietnam 172
Grover Mullins, WWII, ETO 176
William Murray, WWII, ETO 178
William Paschal, WWII, ETO 182
Walter Pawlesh, WWII, ETO 186
Alvar Platt WWII, ETO 188
John Playter, WWII, PTO 192
J. Charles Plumb, Vietnam 194
Murray Pritchard, WWII, ETO 198
Charles Pruitt, WWII, PTO 200
Benjamin Purcell, Vietnam 202
Dudley Riley, WWII, ETO 204
Norman Rippee, WWII, ETO 206

Robinson Risner, Vietnam 208
Arlo Robb, Korea 210
Zach Roberts, WWII, ETO 214
Ralph Rodriguez, Jr., WWII, PTO 216
John Romine, WWII, ETO 218
Wilburn Rowden, WWII, ETO 220
Clifford Savage, WWII, ETO 224
Allen Seamans, WWII, ETO 226
Roy Shenkel, WWII, ETO 228
Robert Shumaker, Vietnam 230
Ira Simpson, WWII, ETO 234
Ralph Sirianni, WWII ETO 236
Jack Sites, WWII, ETO 238
Edward Slater, Korea 240
John Smith, WWII, ETO 242
William Smith, Korea 244
James Stockdale, Vietnam* 248
James Stone, Korea* 250
Clifford Stumpf, WWII, ETO 252
Wright Swanay, WWII, ETO 254
Nels Tanner, Vietnam 258
Leo Thorsness, Vietnam * 260
Charles Towne, WWII, PTO 264
Merle Turley, WWII, ETO 266
Stanley Tyron, WWII, ETO 268
Maynard Unger, WWII, ETO 272
John Vennink, WWII, ETO 276
Emilio Vizachero, Jr., WWII, ETO 278
Glenn Wade, WWII, ETO 280
Robert Waldrop, WWII, ETO 282
Leonard Wallenmeyer, WWII, ETO 284
Edgar Whitcomb, WWII, PTO 286
John Wilcox, WWII, ETO 290
Steven Woelk, USS Pueblo, North Korea 292
Jack Woodson, WWII, PTO 294
Eugene Wopata, WWII, ETO 296
ETO denotes European Theater of Operations
PTO denotes Pacific Theater of Operations
*Medal of Honor recipient

ix

DEDICATION

This book is dedicated to those men and women who endured more
for the cause of freedom than any other single group,
the American Ex-Prisoner of War.

ACKNOWLEDGMENTS

I want to thank every American who spent time as a Prisoner of War for your service in difficult circumstances. I also want to thank every Ex-POW who offered their "advice for life" and the inspirational stories in this book.

Once again, I must thank and acknowledge my family, Vicki, Tim, Tricia and Josh, for their support of me and the Eagle series books.

I also need to thank Brian and Evergreen Press. Brian, from the very beginning you recognized and believed in the importance of the books.

I want to thank the men from my Wednesday morning MEN WITHOUT FEAR group who reviewed the book manuscript and studied the wisdom of the individuals who offered their advice for life in the Eagle series books. Thanks Adel A., Kurt B., Denny D., Hadley H., Kurt J. and Mike V.

Finally, a very special thanks to Mike Curtis for allowing me to use his sculpture of the Millennium Eagle for the cover of the book. Mike is internationally known as one of the pre-eminent wildlife sculptors in the United States. If you would like to contact him, he can be reached using the following e-mail address & phone number: Mike Curtis, www.mikecurtis.com 208-263-8074.

INTRODUCTION

In the first book of the Eagle series, Ken Davis wrote the following: "My father is an ex-POW and a survivor of the Bataan Death March. During his captivity he saw perfectly healthy men die because they had no reason to live. They gave up hope. He also saw men who were at death's threshold live to be liberated and enjoy long healthy lives. These men had a reason to live."

"When there is nothing left but God, that is when you realize that God is all you need!"

This book offers "advice for life" and "inspirational stories" from Ex-POWs. These individuals lost their freedom, many were tortured, their emotional and physical health affected, yet they came away from the experience with a better understanding of what is important in life.

When I seek true wisdom or when I try to determine my priorities in life, I find the best answers come from those who have suffered, those who have lost almost everything. When all you have left is hope and faith, you have a keen appreciation of the blessings that come with life. Most of the individuals in this book were able to move from the depth of loss to the zenith of knowledge about what was truly important.

Zechariah 9:12, says "Return to the fortress, ye prisoners of hope: even today do I declare double unto thee." I know of no other group with greater wisdom for life than the Ex-Prisoners of War. These men and women paid a great price for that wisdom.

—*Colonel Jim Coy (Ret.)*

Each individual who participated in this book was asked for a photograph, their advice for life, and an inspirational story.

Their advice for life might be a creed or code of conduct, a motto for life or the advice they would offer their children and grandchildren.

Lieutenant Colonel Carey Ashcraft
U.S. Army (Ret.) • WWII • ETO

My advice to others is this: Never stop trying. Continue to reach ahead and higher. If someone else could do something, I believed that I could learn to do it also. Always be honest, have faith in God, let prayer be part of your daily life. Wisdom is the principal goal, therefore get wisdom and receive understanding. I would also like to encourage others to read daily from the Psalms and Proverbs.

THERE ARE NO ATHEISTS IN FOXHOLES
I had four years of ROTC training at Mississippi State University. Nationwide all ROTC cadets as well as West Point cadets had to accelerate their academic courses during the summer of 1942 to graduate in January 1943.

I graduated in January 1943 and immediately went into the army and OCS at Fort Benning, Georgia. I was eventually assigned to Cannon Company of the 350th Infantry of the 88th Division. We left the United States on November 1, 1943, and were in North Africa before Christmas. From Africa we went to Italy.

On one occasion we came under a heavy mortar barrage. We were unable to find adequate cover. The ground was so hard that we would have had difficulty digging even with tools. We fell to the ground, lying

2

flat, convinced that we had had it. My friend said, "Carey, if you're ever going to do any praying, you better do it now!" Prior to that time, he had indicated that he didn't believe in God. I believe he changed his mind right then and came to the conclusion that there was a God. I guess it's true when they say there are no atheists in foxholes.

I was captured with a small group of soldiers in September, and I was initially moved to Stalag VIIA near Moosberg. After Christmas 1944, we were moved to Oflag 64. In January 1945, we received the news that the Russians were crossing the Vistula River so we had to march five miles to Exin where we were picked up by trains. When we arrived in Exin, however, there were no trains, so we began a 22-kilometer march to Wegheim.

Food was scarce to nonexistent, and over time, I became so weak that I wondered if I would make it. One evening we entered a farm complex. After we received our assignment to sleep in the barn, a Polish man, who worked as slave labor on the farm, took us to where he lived in a small basement. He gave us part of his food, a mush like oatmeal. I was starving and so weak that I am convinced his acts of kindness—giving us a better place to stay and part of his small meal—were the most important ones I ever received.

We were liberated at the end of April, and I traveled by Liberty ship to the United States, arriving in Boston in early June 1945. Even now it is hard to describe the many bitter cold nights on the march, the standing around waiting for roll call, the constant pain of hunger, our constant thoughts of our loved ones—somehow I always believed that I would make it through the war and return home. I also know I was extremely fortunate to survive.

I always knew that my family and my friends were praying for me. It was much later that I found out my father had prayed when he received the telegram stating that I was missing in action. That night the Lord revealed to him in a dream how I was captured.

Kenneth Barney
WWII • ETO

After WWII I was blessed to be called into the ministry. My advice for life is: Put God first, then family, and then love of nation. God is central to my life, but God also intended that I balance this love with a love for my family and for others. Jesus told us in the gospels to love God and to love our neighbor. I have always tried to live with His statement.

No matter what a person does, no matter their occupation, God intends for us to love Him first, but He also expects that we make the love of family a high priority in life. No matter how busy, I always tried to make sure that my wife and children knew that they had a husband and father who loved them and would be there for them.

Today, many men believe that a real man doesn't show tenderness, emotions and love. This is wrong. Real men should and real men do demonstrate their love of God, of family, their neighbors, and the nation.

I want my children, their children, and those who follow after them to know the importance of loving God, family, your neighbor, and this great nation.

GRACE, GRACE, GOD'S GRACE

On May 31, 1944, my bomber and crew were shot down over the Ploesti oil fields of Romania. We were part of the 723rd Squadron, 450th

Bomb Group, 15th Air Force, stationed near Manduria, Italy. Ploesti was one of the most heavily defended targets in Europe because Hitler needed the oil and gasoline for his Wehrmacht. We were short on fighter cover because so much of it was going to England for the coming invasion.

As our B-24 Liberator flew over the target, we lost an engine from flak, which was terrifyingly heavy. We could not keep up with our formation with only three engines, so we fell farther and farther behind the groups that originally followed us. Eventually we were like a sitting duck, flying all alone, and 12 enemy fighters jumped on us. Our gunners shot down two of them, but the odds were too great and we had to bail out.

Not all of the crew bailed out at the same moment, so we were scattered all over the sky. I was by myself, but off in the distance I could see white specks of three of my crew's parachutes. I landed in a plowed field and was quickly captured by Romanian soldiers, who were accompanied by a number of peasants from their village who had seen my chute in the sky.

The soldier who found me lying in a furrow on my stomach was obviously frightened and kept saying, "Explosif! Explosif!" Apparently he had been warned that we carried explosives with us, so he took anything from me that he thought might be a bomb (at least that was my supposition).

I was carrying a New Testament in the leg pocket of my coveralls, and for some reason, the soldier took it. Suddenly I felt sheer panic at the thought of being without a Bible and began trying to make him understand that I wanted it back. Finally he understood my gestures and said, "Testa-ment?" I responded, "Yes, Testa-ment!" He handed it back, and I will always remember the relief I felt. There were some things I could do without, but not the Bible.

The Romanians transported me in a one-horse cart to the little town of Costesti, and the shock of being suddenly alone in a strange land began to settle over me. Later in the day, my pilot, co-pilot and nose gunner were brought to Costesti by train. After spending three days there, three of us were taken by car to the city of Pitesti where we stayed two weeks before being taken by train to Bucharest.

A teen-age Romanian boy began to visit us, and it was surprising how well we were able to communicate despite the language barrier. On June 7, he had a very sober expression, and he showed us a newspaper with the headline, "Invasion." No news could have been more welcome, even though the information was very limited. We never doubted that our forces would go on to victory.

Our deepest concern now was about our families. We knew that the government would wait two weeks before sending telegrams stating that we were missing in action. So, on June 14th, all I could do was think about what my wife would be going through when the doorbell rang and the message was handed to her.

What comforted me most was remembering a conversation I had with her just before leaving. That day, the words of Psalm 91:7 had suddenly flashed into my mind as clearly as if the Lord had spoken audibly to me: "A thousand shall fall at thy side and ten thousand at thy right hand, but it shall not come nigh thee." I had taken my wife aside and shared this assurance with her, saying, "If you ever get a telegram that I am missing in action, you can be sure I am a prisoner and not dead." I never dreamed it would actually happen, but when it did, I realized that the Lord had prompted me to prepare her for my experience.

To this day I cannot read Psalm 91:7 without getting goose bumps. Those bumps are just as large when I read another verse that leaped out at me just before we flew our first mission, and I was having a weak feeling in the pit of my stomach: "O God the Lord, the strength of my salvation, thou hast covered my head in the day of battle" (Psalm 140:7). How real the Scriptural promise turned out to be!

One night just before we went to bed, there was a report that was both encouraging and ominous. The Russians were about 180 miles from Bucharest and had started to move. A number of Romanians had told us they would welcome the British or Americans with open arms, but hated the Russians so deeply that they would fight for Bucharest street by street. As the Red Army drew ever closer, we could imagine ourselves in the middle of the battle.

Then one night the news we most wanted to hear burst like a bombshell, although we did not know everything leading up to it until we got home and read the news accounts. King Michael had summoned the Fascist dictator Antonescu to the palace to discuss an armistice with the Russians. When Antonescu hesitated, Michael had him locked in a vault while he signed the armistice.

Our celebrating was cut short by the savage revenge bombing the Luftwaffe rained on Bucharest for the next several days. The Nazis still held the airfields around the city, which meant their bombing runs were frequent, and our nerves soon became very frayed.

The Romanian authorities evacuated us to a garrison in the country—a welcome relief from the strain of diving under tables when the bombers came over. Finally our senior officer was allowed to use their short wave radio to contact the 15th Air Force headquarters in Bari, Italy. A few days later, a sizable number of B-17s landed at an airfield near Bucharest. These planes were converted temporarily to provide space to carry us to freedom and were accompanied by a swarm of P-51 Mustangs. Early in the morning, we were trucked to the air field and returned to Bari. After going through the necessary processing, we were sent to Naples and then to New York by ship.

I cannot find the words to describe my homecoming. I arrived home in Topeka, Kansas, on Sunday afternoon, and we went to our church, First Assembly of God, that night. When we opened the door to enter, the congregation was singing, "Grace, grace, God's grace." Nothing could have been more fitting. It was indeed by God's grace that I was home without a scratch. Why I was spared when two of my crew were not is something I cannot answer. I only know it puts a greater responsibility on us survivors to make the most of the life that has been given us.

William Bearisto
WWII • ETO
Past National Commander
American Ex-POW Association, 1993-1994

To get ahead in life, it is very important to continue your education. Without an education, it is very difficult to be successful. Practicality, hard work, persistence and a positive attitude can help to overcome many obstacles in life. Finally, maybe most importantly…always be honest.

Always put your faith first. Faith in God carried me through my experience as a POW. I believe my trust in God kept me alive.

GIVE THANKS

I was a prisoner of war, captured in Germany in December 1944 at the Battle of the Bulge. By the age of 19 I had already served in four major campaigns.

I lost my freedom when I was captured. My concern about my future and what would happen caused me great distress. I did not know if I would live or die. Food was very scarce, and I lost 60 pounds during my imprisonment.

I frequently prayed that I would survive and live to see my family again. My faith in God helped me to carry on and survive. I looked forward to the time when I would be free again and return home to my family.

After joining the American Ex-Prisoners of War Association, I worked through the ranks to become the National Commander. This was a very rewarding experience. Later I became the President of the American Ex-Prisoners of War Service Foundation.

I was blessed with a successful business, a great family, and a wife who truly cared. Every day I give thanks to God for allowing me to be free in the greatest country in the world, the United States of America!

Paul Bergman
WWII • ETO

My advice for life is to always do what you know is right. Knowing what is right and doing what is right are two different things. Always stand up for what you believe in, even when it is difficult and unpopular. I would also encourage you to have faith in God. We read in Hebrews 11:6, "Without faith it is impossible to please Him." I also believe it is important to treat everyone the way you would want to be treated.

TOUGH DECISION

I was working in a grocery store in Tulsa, Oklahoma, in 1942. My mother, younger sister and brother, and my wife and I were all living together in a large house. My oldest brother was single and living in California. The Army was about to draft him into the service when he wrote to my mother and invited her to come to California and live with him. The decision to stay or to move was extremely tough on her because she knew whether she stayed or moved, one of her sons would be drafted because of it. She moved to California, and I enlisted into the Army Air Corps.

I became a radioman on a B-24 Bomber attached to the 93rd Bomb Group of the 409th Bomb Squadron. We were shot down October 9, 1944, over Dawelshausen, Germany. I was liberated April 5, 1945. I was in the hospital and in rehabilitation the entire time due to fractures in my feet and leg. I was fortunate, in some ways, that I did not have to make the forced march because my cast was constantly breaking down and being changed. Every time they changed the cast, they would write a new date on it. When I was shot down and captured, I weighed 195 lbs. By the time I was liberated, I only weighed 127 lbs.

To get shot down, to be captured, and to be injured sure seemed like a lot of bad luck. However it was the injuries that may have helped save my life.

Lieutenant Colonel Robert Bieber
U.S. Air Force (Ret.) • WWII • ETO

I was an aircraft commander on a B-24 flying with the 8th Air Force out of England. On the 17th of January, 1945, our aircraft took a direct hit from an 88-mm anti-aircraft gun over Hamburg, Germany. Three of us were still in the B-24 when it exploded.

I woke up in a small part of the remaining cockpit, falling through the air. I pushed myself clear of the wreckage and pulled my ripcord. When the chute opened, I was no higher than a thousand feet. I saw pieces of my aircraft falling all around me. Even though my parachute was damaged by the fire, I survived the landing.

I couldn't stand up or walk, and spent one week in a German hospital until I was able to walk. Then it was interrogation camp, several POW camps, a forced march from Nuremberg to Moosberg, Stalag Luft VIIA. I was liberated in early May by General Patton's 3rd Army.

I learned how to pray on the January 17, 1945. My prayer was short, "Father in heaven, thank You." I did a lot of praying while a POW. Most of my prayers were for protection from the harm all around us, and then thanking God for survival. My experience, being in the aircraft when it exploded and surviving as a POW, taught me two things: First, I learned that God is alive and in His heaven. He is good, He listens, and He answers. Second, when I ask Him for help, I must expect Him to help. I must not doubt that my prayers will be answered. This positive attitude is very important when praying. I must enthusiastically believe my prayers will be answered.

"Ask, and it shall be given to you; seek, and you shall find; knock, and it shall be opened to you" (Matthew 7:7).

Ever since 1945, I have applied these two lessons to my life. Through good times and bad, in good health and through two bouts with cancer, and during unbelievable difficult circumstances, they have never failed me!

WHY ME?

During WWII I was a pilot of a B-24 Liberator. On January 17, 1945, our bomber took a direct hit from an anti-aircraft gun. I looked back and saw the aircraft was on fire. Through the intercom, I told everyone to bail out. I repeated the message several times.

I must have been knocked unconscious. When I came to, I was on a small piece of the wreckage from the aircraft. I concluded that the aircraft must have exploded while I was trying to get all the crewmembers to bail out. I pulled and pushed the wreckage away from me and pulled the rip-cord of my parachute. When the parachute opened, I was in a horizontal position, and the force of the opening of the chute and the sudden stop broke my neck. I lost consciousness again, probably falling 20,000 feet before I regained consciousness. The landing was hard, but I survived. Several members of my crew were killed. I asked myself, "Why did God save me? Why me?"

After several months as a POW in Germany, enduring extreme cold, very little food, and a 95-mile forced march, I was liberated on April 29, 1945. Because I was a "short timer," I did not leave Germany until the 10th of May. The C-47 loaded our group (27 ex-POWs) and started flying for Camp Lucky Strike in France. During the flight, the Flight Engineer told us the aircraft was out of fuel and we were going to have to crash-land. The pilot landed, wheels-up, in a small pasture. As soon as we could get the door open, we jumped out and ran as far from the plane as we could. The aircraft did not explode or burn, so we were able to go back to the plane to get our personal belongings. The seat where I was sitting was gone, and we could see a part of a propeller had broken off and had entered the fuselage where I had been sitting.

I had previously picked up and was carrying a German dress bayonet as a souvenir and was wearing it on the right side of my belt. Someone said, "Bieb, look at your bayonet!" The bayonet was bent in a 45-degree angle and was marked with paint from the blade of the propeller. That bayonet probably saved my life or at least my right leg. I thought, *God did it again*. I wondered what He was saving me for and asked again, "Why me?"

I was able to get on a ship at Le Havre bound for New York City. Halfway home, in the mid-afternoon during very rough seas, I experienced pain on my right side. I reported to sick call, and the only doctor on board examined me. After a number of tests, he concluded that I had acute appendicitis, and I needed immediate surgery. By that time, it was dark and the storm had increased in its intensity. The doctor, who was a GP, and the medical corpsman, who had been drafted as a pre-med student prior to medical school, started the surgery. The physician gave me spinal anesthesia. Due to my poor physical condition from being a POW and his conservative use of painkillers, I began to vomit during the surgery because the pain was so intense. Because of this they decided to administer an ether anesthetic. The surgery was completed in the middle of the night, with poor lighting, during a raging storm. When we arrived in New York City, I was the last POW to leave the ship. I was transferred to a local hospital. I realized, God had saved me again. "Why me?"

After the war, I went to college on the GI Bill. I was recalled to active duty in August 1947 and was assigned to Strategic Air Command. I continued to fly, got married, had children, read the Bible, went to church, taught Sunday School, and waited for God to tell me why He had saved me. I retired from the USAF in 1960 and started my own company.

In 1994, I was diagnosed with cancer of the tongue. I received radiation therapy, and every day I spent time talking with God. The oncologist said that I was in remission, however, one year later they found nodules in both lungs. The oncologist recommended that I go to the M.D. Anderson Cancer Center in Houston for treatment. I was placed on a new protocol, and each treatment period took three weeks. Again I talked with God every day. After 18 weeks, the doctors concluded that I was once again in remission.

In 1996, I read about the American Ex-Prisoners of War organization. I began to attend monthly meetings in Colorado Springs and became a member of the organization. Because of my background and my profession, the national organization asked me to be the Chairman of the National Education Committee in 1997. Since then, I have helped direct AXPOW Association speakers all over the United States, having them speak to school children, civic clubs, and military units about their experiences. We seek to stress the importance of a positive attitude and a firm belief in the power of God and the power of prayer. We might ask, "Why me?" But we need to conclude that God does have a plan and purpose for our lives.

Donald Boyer
WWII • ETO

I grew up on the farm. We were up by 5:00 AM every morning milking the cows. From that experience I learned the value of hard work. After milking the cows and doing my morning chores, I walked to school. From my family I also learned the importance of the Golden Rule, to treat others the same way that you would want to be treated. I also learned the importance of truth and honesty. We lived by the teachings of the Bible, and it is the advice that I would offer to others. In life, put God first, then country, and both above self.

LAND OF THE FREE

In November 1944, I turned 20. In two short months I found myself on the front line and was captured by the German army in what is now called the Battle of the Bulge.

We had heard that the Germans were taking no prisoners, and once captured, we felt all was lost. The Germans rounded us up and made us stand in a straight line. One of their tanks moved into the area and pointed the machine gun directly at us! We stood there for a very, very long time. I thought about our farm in Platte City, Missouri, my girlfriend, my buddies back home, and the Friday night football games—win or lose, the whole town turned out. Funny thing, I couldn't wait to get out of that hick town, and at that moment in Germany I would have given everything I had to be back there, helping Dad do the daily chores. One gets to thinking of the very ordinary things in life and just how special they can be when you think you'll never be able to experience them again.

After approximately four or five hours, we made a run for the woods. I was shot in the back of the head but survived—others were not so lucky. We thought that was bad, but our journey to hell was only just beginning as the Germans marched us to a waiting train to take us to our final destination—Stalag XIB. We were housed there with no heat, no water, an outside toilet, and very little food. We were beaten and questioned again and again—living on a farm in Platte City, Missouri, was looking better and better all the time. God has a plan for us. We might not know what it is, but I thank God for giving me another chance to live in this wonderful land of the free, the United States of America.

Vernon Brooks
WWII • ETO

In February, 1942, I was called to defend my country. I received my training at Fort Lewis, Washington, and then went to Boston where I shipped to France.

I was captured in 1945 in France by the Germans. We moved a lot, never staying in one place for any length of time. They moved us a lot in boxcars the Germans called 40 and 8—which meant that they would hold 40 men and eight horses. Food was scarce. We usually got one potato each day, and sometimes a stale slab of bread. After being held prisoner for four months, I was liberated by my fellow countrymen. During the time I was held prisoner, I asked the Lord several times to get me home safely. My prayers were answered.

My mother gave me a small Bible when I left home for basic training. I carried it with me at all times. My oldest grandson asked for the Bible when he graduated from high school so he could take it to college with him. When I gave it to him, he remarked, "Grandpa, it got you through the war and home safely. I will carry it to college to help me on my way."

Upon my release from the Army, I started farming and spent my life tilling the soil. It seemed like the most peaceful occupation. I thank the Lord that I made it through the war and am still here with my family.

THANK THE LORD!

I was born in Sturgeon, Missouri, one of 11 children. Three of the boys went into the service during WWII. All three of us returned home. I was one of the lucky ones in that I returned home, but unlucky because I was captured during the Battle of the Bulge, January 1, 1945. I was assigned to the 44th Division with the 324th infantry. A lot of things happened that day. I remember bullets flying all around me and the soldiers that I was with. Some of us survived; many did not. We were captured and then transported from camp to camp in boxcars that would hold 40 men and eight horses. To me, it seemed like most times we were put in the boxcars immediately after the horses came out. We could hear the planes overhead while we were in the boxcars, and we would pray that we would not be bombed. I carried a small Bible in my pocket, and I always felt that Someone was watching over me. Some of the food that we ate was from scraps swept up from the floor. We used the scraps to make soup. At times we were able to steal beets and supplement our food intake. I was blessed because I was never really mistreated. I arrived home in December 1945, and I continue to thank the Lord every day because He allowed me to make it home safely!

Colonel William Byrns
U.S. Air Force (Ret.) • Vietnam

The military trains us mentally and physically to be leaders. It truly is the best training in the world. The key to successful leadership is the development of the spiritual part of our being. I have noticed, over my 30 years of service, that the most outstanding leaders I have met have a deep faith in God. Some of those leaders have had to lead under extremely adverse conditions such as in combat and in a prisoner of war situation. The North Vietnamese were able to eventually weaken us mentally and physically but could not weaken us spiritually. Without Jesus Christ as my Lord and Savior, I could not have made it. The core values of integrity, service, and excellence are critical to leadership and can be absolute when we are mentally, physically, and spiritually developed as leaders. The combination then produces character. Character is doing the right thing when no one else, except God, is looking.

THE TASTE OF FREEDOM

It was the afternoon of May 23, 1972, at Ubon Air Base, Thailand. My weapon systems Operator, Captain Ray Bean and I briefed the combat mission and proceeded to our F-4D Phantom. On the way I met a high school classmate of mine who had landed with battle damage. I had not seen Doug Holmes for many years. It is a small world considering we only had 67 members in our class. After visiting briefly, goodbyes were said and I pressed on with the intended mission, not knowing I would not see Doug again for a year and a half.

There were no problems with the flight up until the shoot-down. We were on a five hour flight with numerous air-to-air refuelings. The mission was scheduled as a FAC (Forward Air Controller) mission into North Vietnam. Our job was to find targets (trucks, tanks, artillery, etc.) and direct fire on them from airborne fighters. We were able to locate enemy trucks and tanks moving toward South Vietnam. Our area of operation was Route Pack I, about 15 miles north of the Demilitarized Zone and about ten miles inland from the coast. SAMs (Surface to Air Missiles) were fired at us as well as the flight of F-4s we were working with in the target area. We had to jink (maneuver) numerous times to avoid being hit, but finally we were hit by 57-MM anti-aircraft fire. Our aircraft caught fire and began spinning out of control. After making a Mayday call, I said we were getting out of the aircraft, and I ejected both of us.

It was already dusk and hard for the enemy to see our parachutes; however, they still shot at us as we descended to earth. I would not see Ray again for three days. When I hit the ground, I went through all the survival procedures that I had been taught. The next step after landing was to hide my parachute and find a good place to hide myself. At this time I made a call on my survival radio to let the friendly fighters overhead know that I was down and okay. The terrain was rough with bomb craters and small hills. The only real cover was thick brush about six to ten feet high. I found a good place to hide in a huge bush with a hollowed out area and I dug in.

After getting settled in my hiding place, I again contacted the fighter overhead, and they were able to determine my exact position. I could hear enemy soldiers searching for us and saw them shooting in the bushes at other positions. They were trying to frighten me, and it was working fairly well. I pulled out the 38-caliber revolver that each of us carried. The first chamber of the cylinder of the revolver was kept empty for safety reasons. The squadron commander ordered that the first bullet be removed because of an accident in the squadron when a pilot accidentally shot himself in the thigh. As I pulled the pistol from the holster, I quickly realized a gun fight with a multitude of enemy soldiers was futile. I holstered the weapon and then proceeded to try to make contact again with the rescue forces and was told that they were trying to get helicopters into the area for our rescue.

As it grew darker and night settled in, word came that there was too much anti-aircraft fire and SAMs to allow a rescue, and it would be first light before any further attempt could be made. The news was devastating, and hope of rescue seemed gone. My stomach felt like it fell to my toes, and I quickly realized that I had been putting my hope and faith in the power of the United States and all the military forces available to them in this area of the world to rescue me.

I had accepted Jesus Christ as my Savior when I was in college through the ministry of the Fellowship of Christian Athletes. My spiritual growth continued through Officer's Christian Fellowship and Campus Crusade for Christ Bible studies. Because Jesus was the Lord of my life, I was aware that He was the only solid rock on which to stand. I cried out to God during this devastating situation and told Him that I did not want to die here and that I wanted to see my family again, but I would also accept His will for me in this situation. Calmness and peace came over me and remained throughout the night and even throughout my capture and the period of time that I was held as a prisoner of war. There were times that I was beaten and tortured and the situation was bleak, but that peace never left me. I realized that this was not of my power, but was supernatural power. God, not the circumstances, was in control of my life.

I continued to make contact with rescue forces throughout the night. Apparently the enemy had surrounded me, and a North Vietnamese soldier stepped on me. As I reached up to grab him, I realized that I was surrounded by about 15-20 enemy soldiers with AK-47 rifles pointed at me. The soldier took a club and began to beat me with it. I was beaten so badly that I was unable to use my arm for three weeks. When the beating stopped, another soldier grabbed my pistol out of the holster, held it to my head, and pulled the trigger. The weapon did not fire! Before he could pull the trigger a second time, another soldier grabbed the gun from the hand of the soldier who had tried to kill me. God was faithful even in the small details. I had obeyed the order to keep the first round in the cylinder empty, and that obedience and the grace of God saved my life. I was then stripped of my flight suit and boots, blindfolded, tied up, and walked all night with enemy soldiers to a bunker. It took almost one month to reach Hanoi, traveling by boat and truck. Most of the time I was tied up, handcuffed, or in leg irons. Two other POWs, including Ray, were captured along the way and were transported with me.

Once we arrived in Hanoi, I was placed in solitary confinement for a period of time and eventually was placed with three cellmates. The conditions were primitive, with poor food, some torture, and rampant sickness. However, God was ever present and gave us hope, peace, and strength. The pistol that did not fire was not the only miracle that happened in that prison. Scratched on the wall of my first cell in Hoa Lo Prison (Hanoi Hilton) was the statement: "Freedom has a taste for those who have fought and almost died for it, that the protected shall never know." I claimed the promise of God from His Word: "If God be for us, who can be against us?" (Romans 8:31)

When the peace agreement was signed and we were released to our countrymen, it was like a giant weight was lifted off me. The oppression of captivity gave me a fresh awareness of what true freedom is all about. While in prison, I realized that I had taken my freedoms for granted all my life and was determined upon my return home to read the Constitution and fully understand the oath that I had taken to defend it. After reading it, I learned that God and liberty are the basis and moral compass of the United States of America. The promises of "Blessed is the nation whose God is the Lord" (Psalm 33:12) and "Where the Spirit of the Lord is, there is liberty" (II Corinthians 3:17) give us a standard for our people and our nation.

The enemy was able to take away my physical freedom and to make me feel like I was at the end of my mental and emotional rope, but they could not take away my spiritual freedom, which was in God's control. I realized then that the rights and freedoms in the Declaration of Independence are God-given, not given by man. Thus, only God could take them away or we can freely give them up. Jesus said: "I will never leave thee, nor forsake thee" (Hebrews 13:5). I claimed the promise then and still do today. God bless America!

23

Robert Carter
WWII • ETO

When I was growing up, my dad taught me to do the best in whatever I had undertaken. This gave me pride in my work and increased my determination to always do my best. I taught the same thing to my daughter and son who both demonstrate a wonderful work ethic. They also have a love for God in everything they do. With perseverance, faith, and trust in God, almost nothing is impossible.

KEEP PRAYING

I entered the service on September 14, 1943, and was assigned to the 15th Air Force, the 464th Bomb Group and the 777th Squadron. On January 20, 1945, we were shot down. A few weeks after I returned home from the war, my dad told me that my mother woke up one night crying. She said she knew something had happened to me. He was unable to console her and the next day the family called our pastor, asking him to come to our home. He told her, "The Lord works in mysterious ways. Keep praying for your son's safe return." The incident happened the very same day that I was shot down. It changed my life forever.

Sergeant Major Jon Cavaiani
U.S. Army (Ret.) • Vietnam
Medal of Honor

If I were to offer my advice about a creed or code of conduct for life and about success and significance, I would offer the advice given to me by my father. When I asked him how he became a success, he told me, "Honesty and making the right decisions were the major factors that helped me through life." He also said that before he made a decision to do something, he asked himself three simple questions: "Will what I do hurt my family?" "Will it hurt my friends?" And finally, "Will it hurt me?" He said if he can answer yes to any of these questions, he wouldn't do it. He believed your word is your bond. I have lived by these words throughout my life.

CITATION

S/Sgt. Cavaiani distinguished himself by conspicuous gallantry and intrepidity at the risk of life above and beyond the call of duty in action in the Republic of Vietnam on 4 and 5 June 1971 while serving as a platoon leader to a security platoon, providing security for an isolated radio relay site located within enemy-held territory.

On the morning of 4 June 1971, the entire camp came under an intense barrage of enemy small arms, automatic weapons, rocket-propelled grenade and mortar fire from a superior size enemy force. S/Sgt. Cavaiani acted with complete disregard for his personal safety as he repeatedly exposed himself to heavy enemy fire in order to move about the camp's perimeter directing the platoon's fire and rallying the platoon in a desperate fight for survival. S/Sgt. Cavaiani also returned heavy suppressive fire upon the assaulting enemy force during this period with a variety of weapons. When the entire platoon was to be evacuated, S/Sgt. Cavaiani unhesitatingly volunteered to remain on the ground and direct the helicopters into the landing zone. S/Sgt. Cavaiani was able to direct the first 3 helicopters in evacuating a major portion of the platoon. Due to intense increase in enemy fire, S/Sgt. Cavaiani was forced to remain at the camp overnight where he calmly directed the remaining platoon members in strengthening their defenses.

On the morning of 5 June, a heavy ground fog restricted visibility. The superior size enemy force launched a major ground attack in an attempt to completely annihilate the remaining small force. The enemy force advanced in 2 ranks, first firing a heavy volume of small arms automatic weapons and rocket-propelled grenade fire while the second rank continuously threw a steady barrage of hand grenades at the beleaguered force. S/Sgt. Cavaiani returned a heavy barrage of small arms and hand grenade fire on the assaulting enemy force but was unable to slow them down. He ordered the remaining platoon members to attempt to escape while he provided them with cover fire. With one last courageous exertion, S/Sgt. Cavaiani recovered a machine gun, stood up, completely exposing himself to the heavy enemy fire directed at him, and began firing the machine gun in a sweeping motion along the 2 ranks of advancing enemy soldiers. Through S/Sgt. Cavaiani's valiant efforts with complete disregard for his safety, the majority of the remaining platoon members were able to escape. While inflicting severe losses on the advancing enemy force, S/Sgt. Cavaiani was wounded numerous times.

S/Sgt. Cavaiani's conspicuous gallantry, extraordinary heroism and intrepidity at the risk of his life, above and beyond the call of duty, were in keeping with the highest traditions of the military service and reflect great credit upon himself and the U.S. Army.

Colonel Robert Certain
U.S. Air Force (Ret.) • Vietnam

My wisdom for life is: JOY = Jesus first, Others second, Yourself last. My spiritual advice: Walk in love as Christ loved us and gave Himself for us.

THE CHAINS OF FEAR, DOUBT AND GRIEF

In my book, *Unchained Eagle: From Prisoner of War to Prisoner of Christ*, I described my experience as a prisoner of war. My life didn't begin in Vietnam, but it didn't end there either. Through the grace of God, I was repatriated, at least in part. Though the cell doors had opened and the Starlifter had flown me out of that terrible place, the chains of the past continued to have a very long reach, snapping me back into the dungeons of a dark night of the soul, often when my life events were at their most expectant. I frequently felt like the eagle depicted on the shield of the 4th Allied P.O.W. Wing with wings spread for flight, but the shackle and chain were holding me down. Only after decades of struggling with continued meaning of the events of the winter of 1972-73 were my eyes finally opened to recognize that the chain was no longer connected to a post, that while its weight might continue to affect my perspective, it no longer had the power to imprison me. As I worked to commit this story to print, another more ancient story kept coming to mind.

In the Gospel of Luke 24:13-35 there is an intriguing story that speaks of the filling of memory and the enlightenment of understanding. Two of Jesus' disciples, Cleopas and a companion, were returning from Emmaus on Easter Day. They had been walking with Jesus for several miles, talking with Him, not knowing who He was until He broke the bread at dinner. Suddenly, their eyes were opened, and they recognized Jesus. The trip from Jerusalem to Emmaus was a trip of despair and hopelessness, as far as they knew when the trip started out. It was only when they recognized the Lord in Emmaus, at the close of the day, that they finally realized the trip was really a walk with the Lord.

I have been very much like those two men in my own tragedies, and sometimes even in my inconveniences, in failing to ask where Jesus could possibly be. Many of my plans have not turned out the way I envisioned them, and out of the depths, I have cried for the Lord to open the eyes of my faith that I might behold Him in all His redeeming work.

I was trained in seminary in theological reflection, but it has been a daily chore to apply that training. Writing this story set me on the road to Emmaus, walking with the Lord as He explained the passages of my life that showed His hand at work. I had always seen many parts of my life as a diversion from the ministry, and so much of it as painful and outside the realm of redemption.

Through the ministry of a young Christian psychologist at the San Bernardino Vet Center, I was sent back in time to reevaluate events that I had understood to be "coincidence." She said, "Go back and read your story again, and instead of seeing only coincidence, ask yourself if God was working in every part of that story, not just the parts you wanted Him to be working in." Through the subsequent ministry of a Christian family counselor in Riverside, California, I finally glimpsed the light of Christ shining before me on the path in my darkest nights of the soul.

In committing this story to the written word, I realized that throughout my life my heart had burned within me in places where I did not want to return. When I went there, I found that Christ was walking beside me all the way, carrying the keys that would eventually free me from my chains of fear, doubt, and grief. I do not believe that I am any different from any other pilgrims along the way, and certainly no different from Cleopas and his companion.

29

In Psalm 116:10, the question is asked, "How shall I repay the Lord for all the good things he has done for me?" Anyone can read all the answers of the Scriptures, but only the individual can read his or her own life. Only pilgrims can go back into their own journeys from Jerusalem to Emmaus to discover how Jesus has walked with them in ways they did not understand.

Looking again at the tapestry of life and seeing the hand of God working in every thread, my eyes have been opened to His redeeming work in surprising places. Tragedies have become times of God's imminent presence, and coincidences and the routine events of daily life form the intricate design of God's hand at work in the world. Perhaps now I can understand and experience the fullness of joy that is found in the people and events that I have called blessings. But even more, I now realize God's hand at work in those events and relationships that I had once locked so securely in my closet of unredeemable things.

While the road I have taken may be unique in the details and in the footsteps I have left behind, the themes of dark nights and glorious days are common to us all. By looking back at the stories of our lives, perhaps we can see more clearly where we are heading in whatever future God has granted us.

Psalm 23

The LORD is my shepherd; I shall not want.

He maketh me to lie down in green pastures: he leadeth me beside the still waters.

He restoreth my soul: he leadeth me in the paths of righteousness for his name's sake.

Yea, though I walk through the valley of the shadow of death, I will fear no evil: for thou art with me; thy rod and thy staff they comfort me.

Thou preparest a table before me in the presence of mine enemies: thou anointest my head with oil; my cup runneth over.

Surely goodness and mercy shall follow me all the days of my life: and I will dwell in the house of the LORD for ever.

Colonel Fred Cherry
U.S. Air Force (Ret.) • Vietnam

My seven and a half years as a POW in North Vietnam will always have an impact on my life. I survived the pain, torture, isolation, loneliness, and hopelessness through my faith in God, family, country, fellow prisoners, and self. I relied on my Christian faith to get me through the toughest times. I was thankful for my Christian upbringing and the values which I had been taught by my family, elders, and teachers. When all hope seemed to fade and creep away, my faith would grasp the fading hope and reel it back within my reach. Without the sound values deeply imbedded in me, my performance as an American fighting man in the hands of the enemy would have been miserable and so would my ability to face myself in a mirror today.

We must continue to teach our young people the sound values which have been the foundation for all great people and nations. Our youth are our future, and the survival of our nation will depend on leadership. We must develop leaders with unwavering integrity, honesty, moral character, and love. Young Americans: Have faith, set your goals high, and aspire to be the best that you can be. Build your foundation on the values that have made great men, women, and nations

HONOR, INTEGRITY, FAITH IN GOD

I am an authentic American citizen of Native American and African heritage. I grew up in a rural area of Virginia, near Suffolk, the youngest of eight children. There were four boys and four girls. We were a very close family. It seemed as though everyone in the neighborhood were members of one big family. The neighbors felt responsible to help rear and raise everyone else's kids. My family was a religious family so we were in the Baptist church every Sunday. All during my youth I was taught what was right and what was wrong, and I was expected to always do what was right.

I was very young when I first had a desire to fly. During WWII, my home was near a Navy auxiliary base that was used to practice carrier landings on a regular runway. As a young boy, I would often watch these planes, and my desire to become a pilot grew. About the same time, the Tuskegee Airmen shipped to Italy and North Africa. The story of these heroes only increased my desire to fly, although my family always thought and maybe hoped I would become a doctor.

After high school I went to college and I took all the tests to see if I could join the Air Force and become a pilot. I was accepted, then enlisted in the Air Force, awaited assignment to flight training, completed my training, and was commissioned a second lieutenant. In a short period of time, I began flying combat missions in Korea and flew over 50 combat sorties during the Korean War.

After the Korean War, I remained in the Air Force, and seven years later, I was assigned to Japan for five years. In 1965 I flew combat missions over North Vietnam. I was flying a F-105 Thunder Chief out of Thailand when I was shot down in October 1965. When my aircraft was hit by anti-aircraft fire, the cockpit began to fill with smoke. The plane exploded and I ejected at about 400 feet at over 600 miles an hour. In the process of ejection, I broke my left ankle, my left wrist, and crushed my left shoulder. I was captured immediately upon landing by Vietnamese militia and civilians. Thus began my seven and a half years as a prisoner of war. I experienced some very brutal treatment. I spent 702 days in solitary confinement, the longest period of time was for 53 weeks. At one time I was either tortured or in punishment for 93 straight days.

During my life I have certainly experienced some memorable times. I believe good conquers evil, and that there is no substitute for honor, integrity, love, and faith. I am convinced that faith in God, country, our fellow man, and one's self will help to overcome any situation during the toughest of times.

I know that the faith in God, and love and respect for my fellow man that my parents and family instilled in me during my youth carried me through some very difficult years as a POW in Vietnam. I was always taught to love and respect others and forgive those who mistreat, scorn, or persecute me. Righteousness will prevail, and evil will be overcome.

That same love, honor, integrity, respect, faith, and will to forgive have always guided me in every endeavor and walk of life. They have allowed me to overcome the damages of discrimination, Jim Crow, and the social and economic barriers associated with growing up a poor dirt farmer.

We have choices to make in life. We need to be concerned that we make the right choices. I strongly advocate that every choice we make be based upon some standard. My standard for making decisions is based on doing what is right, or what some might call, "doing the right thing." I use as my embedded standard: honor, integrity, faith in God and country, and love. Believe that right will prevail over wrong. Know that honor, integrity, faith in God and country, respect, and love will set you free.

The Lord's Prayer

Our Father which art in heaven, Hallowed be thy name. Thy kingdom come. Thy will be done in earth, as it is in heaven. Give us this day our daily bread. And forgive us our debts, as we forgive our debtors. And lead us not into temptation, but deliver us from evil: For thine is the kingdom, and the power, and the glory, for ever. Amen.   —Matthew 6:9-13

Howard Chrisco
WWII • PTO

I am a humble World War II soldier who experienced the atrocious and brutal acts committed against the United States forces during the "Death March" in the Philippines. I was a prisoner for 15 months before escaping and living with Filipino guerrillas for ten months. Through short-wave radio, we made contact with the submarine, Crevalle, which returned me to Australia.

My survival as a prisoner was only possible because of my strong will to live and my personal faith in God. Still, at times, I wasn't sure I would make it. These experiences strengthened my faith in God, and today, I often find myself thanking Him for watching over me and caring for me.

My wartime experiences certainly taught me how precious life is and impacted my living. I like to set goals and work until those goals are accomplished. I believe that honesty along with treatment of my fellow man as I want to be treated are important attributes to honor. Because of my experiences, I have a very positive outlook on life. God has been good to me, and I am grateful for the many years of health and happiness with my wife of 56 years and our two sons and their families.

HAPPY BIRTHDAY

After the war I would jokingly tell people that I spent one birthday in the American Army, one birthday in the Japanese Army, and one birthday in the Philippine Army. After I was rescued and returned to the United States, I had not told my family when I was coming home. I wanted to surprise them on my 25th birthday.

It was after midnight when I reached the small town of Salem, Missouri. Stopping in front of the small, white house, I headed to the door and knocked. After a while I saw a light go on in the back of the house; my father appeared in the hallway. When he saw me standing at the door, he didn't recognize me; he thought I was his nephew. As he stared through the screen, he finally realized it was me. He said, "Howard!" I responded, "I'm home, Dad." He practically tore the door off the hinges.

I asked, "How's Mom?" Dad gave me the bad news. While I was away she had gone blind.

I followed him upstairs and entered their bedroom. Dad said, "Laura, I've got a surprise for you." Then I said, "Mom, I'm home." As she began to cry, I knelt down to give her a hug. As she ran her hand over my head, she whispered, "It's Howard, all right. My prayers have been answered!"

Colonel John Clark
U.S. Air Force (Ret.) • Vietnam

As we proceed through life, we begin to realize that we are less and less significant, and God's creation that abounds around us, often unnoticed, increases in its significance. Our successes, which are usually measured by personal and material accomplishments, will only transcend to significance when we are able to positively influence the lives of others. We also appreciate God's creation more as we realize that we are blessed to be part of it.

A quote engraved on a plaque I received upon departing the unit I commanded filled me with a feeling of significance: "Your wisdom and leadership inspired us to search for excellence." In life, we are all blessed with certain abilities and a free will with which to use those abilities. It is up to each of us to apply those abilities to the greatest good. A strict code of integrity and honesty in our dealings with others is a key to reaching success and significance.

While a POW in North Vietnam for six years and out of touch with the rest of my world, I mentally created a scrapbook of memories of family, friends, events, and things that pleased me, and I reviewed it frequently. In doing this I noticed and remembered things, of which I was not proud, that kept finding a place in my scrapbook. As years passed, my scrapbook became tattered, faded, and some of the pages were missing. I came to realize that the memories that stayed the most vivid were the ones wherein I had made people comfortable or happy. Likewise, I noticed the memories that I regretted most were also slow to fade. I know from that experience and as I reflect on significance in the winter of my life, that my life will be measured by what I have done to cause happiness in the lives and souls of others. And I also know it will be measured by the suffering that I might have caused.

—•••—

THE CROSS

I grew up attending a Christian church in the Midwest and remember well the various church socials and events that we attended as a family, my baptism, and my faith in God and Jesus Christ. As I grew older, matured, and pursued my college education, I noticed a divergence between the teachings of the church and the absolutes of scientific thought and discovery. As I followed my personal aspirations for life, I drifted away from the truth of the church and my faith with little consideration of its teachings.

Some years later I was shot down from the skies of Southeast Asia and a captive of the Communist North Vietnamese who desired information that I was reluctant to give. In short order, the torture convinced me it was time to call upon my forgotten faith, because this was clearly a situation where I needed a greater strength than I possessed.

I prayed and found my prayers hollow. I prayed with all my heart and found no strength, only emptiness. Clearly, my faith had waned. Over a period of gruesome days, I asked myself why had God left me so alone, but I knew the answer before asking: doubt and faithlessness had taken its toll. I had a choice—to endure alone or to find my missing faith and hopefully the inner strength that it might bring. I decided that even though the timing was rather self-serving, my sin would almost certainly be forgiven by an omniscient God if I were sincere in my search for true faith. So the journey began, the journey of rediscovery of faith. I thought perhaps an understanding God might give me a boost with a sign, and I promised in faith that I would try to recognize the sign. I really didn't expect a deep voice from the sky.

I was shot down in March, and the days were damp and cloudy. The cell was cold and dank, and there was a light drizzle in the air, which I could see if I stood on one of the concrete benches that served as a bed. The walls were a moldy, whitewashed stucco with numerous dates, names, initials, and other curious etchings. I noticed that some of the dates were from the French Indo-China period, and I could not help but wonder who of the French Foreign Legion might have shared a similar fate in this cell so far from home. I wondered if they had also betrayed their faith. Had they found the strength to endure an unknown fate?

As I lay on the cold, bare concrete trying not to think of my circumstance, I committed an act that was not allowed by camp regulations—I fell asleep. Some time later, I awoke with a nervous start. Had I been discovered by the roving guard outside the door? It seemed not, but more surprising was the wall at my feet and opposite, the high, narrow, barred window was a stunning white, bathed in a dramatic ray of light shining through the small window. I quickly jumped up and peeked out the window, which revealed a bright setting sun. It slipped under a cloud layer just before it settled out of sight behind the imposing broken glass covered wall of the prison and the Hanoi skyline. So stunning was the patch of white, illuminated wall, that my attention was immediately drawn to it, and just as quickly, I noticed a perfectly etched cross in the center of the ray of light on the wall. I thought I knew everything that was on that wall! I had looked over every inch of it to discover whatever I could, and I had never seen a cross! I reasoned that I had missed it in my pained search, and now a setting sun just happened to illuminate it. Maybe that is why the Christian who etched it there did so. Or was it the "boost" that I had asked for, and would I, as I had promised, have the faith to realize it?

The inner stirring and the tears in my eyes easily conveyed my answer, and my journey back to faith continued with a prayer of thanks and the creation of a story that is still known only to God and to my heart. That cross became the center of my torturous stay in that cell, and it was only the first of several boosts, some not as easily explained. These signs were to mark my path to a new and renewed faith and strength, which I credit for blessing me with a new life.

Psalm 91—The Soldiers' Psalm

He that dwelleth in the secret place of the most High shall abide under the shadow of the Almighty.

I will say of the LORD, He is my refuge and my fortress: my God; in him will I trust.

Surely he shall deliver thee from the snare of the fowler, and from the noisome pestilence.

He shall cover thee with his feathers, and under his wings shalt thou trust: his truth shall be thy shield and buckler.

Thou shalt not be afraid for the terror by night; nor for the arrow that flieth by day;

Nor for the pestilence that walketh in darkness; nor for the destruction that wasteth at noonday.

A thousand shall fall at thy side, and ten thousand at thy right hand; but it shall not come nigh thee.

Only with thine eyes shalt thou behold and see the reward of the wicked.

Because thou hast made the LORD, which is my refuge, even the most High, thy habitation;

There shall no evil befall thee, neither shall any plague come nigh thy dwelling.

For he shall give his angels charge over thee, to keep thee in all thy ways.

They shall bear thee up in their hands, lest thou dash thy foot against a stone.

Thou shalt tread upon the lion and adder: the young lion and the dragon shalt thou trample under feet.

Because he hath set his love upon me, therefore will I deliver him: I will set him on high, because he hath known my name.

He shall call upon me, and I will answer him: I will be with him in trouble; I will deliver him, and honour him.

With long life will I satisfy him, and show him my salvation.

Captain Jerry Coffee
U.S. Navy (Ret.) • Vietnam

My advice for life and my story can be found in my book, *Beyond Survival*. The absolute tests are those we face alone, without the support of others who believe as we do. There the beliefs we hold most dear are challenged—some to be strengthened, some to be tempered, others to be abandoned—but all to be examined. From deep within we claim the values that we know to be our own. Those are the ones by which we are willing to live or die.

When we cannot change a situation, resolution comes through the way we choose to handle it within ourselves. To let go is not to deny, but to accept. Letting go moves us beyond the unproductive lament of, "What if?" and "Why me, Lord?" to the constructive acceptance of, "What is" and "Show me, Lord."

Fear for our survival is a sure sign we're trusting only in our own strength. However we may be in touch with our God, there is great strength in knowing we are never alone. Once that is internalized, every thought, act, concern, project, or challenge has a spiritual dimension. Unlike formal religion, which as often as not divides us, this spiritual dimension connects us with all things.

MY CUP RUNNETH OVER

Every Sunday the senior officer in each cell block would pass a certain signal on the wall—the church call—and wait a few minutes while it circulated. Then every man stood up in his cell—if he was able—and at least in some semblance of togetherness, we would recite the Pledge of Allegiance to our flag, the Lord's Prayer, and frequently the Twenty-third Psalm, focusing on the part that says, "Thou preparest a table before me in the presence of mine enemies. Thou anointest my head with oil. My cup runneth over."

Every time I thought of this, I realized that in spite of the fact that I was incarcerated in that terrible place, I was blessed. I maintained faith that some day, however, whenever, I would return to a beautiful and free country. There was one thing the Vietnamese around me would never know—it was that my cup runneth over.

Colonel J. Quincy Collins
U.S. Air Force (Ret.) • Vietnam

My advice for life is: Know that God is real. He has created us for a purpose that is connected with His Kingdom. Be strong in your benefits and be willing to, step out in support of them. God also created love—an emotion, an action, a passion that no one on earth can ignore. It is habit forming, and it calms the storms of life.

THE GRINCH

The Grinch That Stole Christmas is a popular children's story. It became a reality for us while we were in prison in North Vietnam. It was about 10 days before Christmas and our cell was readying for a Christmas Eve service and other activities. Rod Knutson, a short, feisty guy who looked like James Cagney, had started gathering items to make a Santa Claus outfit. He had been working on this for weeks and weeks. For three months I had been writing arrangements of carols and seasonal songs on big sheets of toilet paper that guys had donated to the cause. The choir rehearsed them and each day I would hide the material—now a pretty big stack.

One day the cell door opened, and we were ordered at gunpoint to get outside. We were panic stricken as everyone was sticking Christmas materials and music in their pants, thinking we would outsmart them! Nah! They ordered us to strip, and Christmas fell on the ground. The guards gathered it up, set it on fire, and had us watch as it disappeared into ashes. Later, in the cell, we moped around—not quite sure what to do. We had a meeting and decided we would accomplish in the next nine days what had taken us months to do.

On Christmas Eve at the appointed time the choir formed, the chaplain took his place, I thumped the B flat tin cup for the key, the new toilet paper music sheets popped up in each choir member's hand, and "Joy to the World" began to resound around the walls in the middle of Hanoi. Suddenly, ladders hit the outside wall as guards showed us their weapons. The choir turned up the volume, the guards looked stunned, shook their heads, and disappeared. Then followed the most meaningful and spiritual Christmas service I have ever witnessed. The Christmas story, its music, and its spirit had defeated our Christmas Grinch. There was truly "Joy to the World."

Charles Crandell
USS Pueblo • North Korea

I grew up in a poor family and learned early the value of hard work in life. From my mother I learned that strength can come from faith in yourself, and with that faith, you can accomplish whatever you set your mind to as long as you are honest and willing to stand by your convictions. As a teenager and as a young man, I realized that working alongside my fellow employees helped me to obtain greater respect than just being the boss.

A BETTER LIFE

We were captured on January 23, 1968, by the North Koreans in international waters. I was wounded while attempting to burn classified material. The last thing on my mind was that I would be captured and held as a POW by the North Koreans. At the time we were at war with North Vietnam, but our ship, the U.S.S. Pueblo, was off the coast of North Korea.

During our captivity we never received any news from our country that we could verify. However, I believed strongly in my country and was convinced that they were working hard to obtain our freedom. Although we went through many long periods of intense interrogation and beatings, my love for my family and my country helped me endure. The desire to be reunited with my family and children was constant.

The faith that my mother always demonstrated when I was young also helped me realize that whether I lived or died, there was a better life that would follow. I believed then and am still convinced that we live in the most compassionate and God-fearing country in the world. I am proud to be an American!

Master Sergeant William Crawford
U.S. Army (Ret.) • WWII • ETO
Medal of Honor

Be the best of whatever you are. I read this poem in a USO library reading room in Algeria. As a private, the poem made me feel worthwhile.

> If you can't be a moon, then just be a star
> But be the best of whatever you are.

This advice is found in the Scriptures, Ecclesiastes 9:10, "Whatsoever thy hand findeth to do, do it with thy might."

CITATION

For conspicuous gallantry and intrepidity at risk of life above and beyond the call of duty in action with the enemy near Altavilla, Italy, 13 September 1943.

When Company I attacked an enemy-held position on Hill 424, the 3d Platoon, in which Pvt. Crawford was a squad scout, attacked as base platoon for the company. After reaching the crest of the hill, the platoon was pinned down by intense enemy machinegun and small-arms fire. Locating one of these guns, which was dug in on a terrace on his immediate front, Pvt. Crawford, without orders and on his own initiative, moved over the hill under enemy fire to a point within a few yards of the gun emplacement and single-handedly destroyed the machinegun and killed three of the crew with a hand grenade, thus enabling his platoon to continue its advance.

When the platoon, after reaching the crest, was once more delayed by enemy fire, Pvt. Crawford again, in the face of intense fire, advanced directly to the front midway between 2 hostile machinegun nests located on a higher terrace and emplaced in a small ravine. Moving first to the left, with a hand grenade he destroyed one gun emplacement and killed the crew; he then worked his way, under continuous fire, to the other and with one grenade and the use of his rifle, killed one enemy and forced the remainder to flee. Seizing the enemy machinegun, he fired on the withdrawing Germans and facilitated his company's advance.

ONLY THE LORD KNOWS

It was the morning of September 13, 1944, near Altavilla, Italy. Several men near me were killed in a flank attack on the German line of defense. I was untouched for some unknown reason. The Lord was looking after me. I accepted the Lord at Stalag IIB in Hammerstein, Germany, in September 1944. At the time, Stalag IIB had received Bibles, hymnals, and an accordion. We organized a "Born Again" evangelistic-type of worship service. We had prayer services every day, and more POWs accepted the Lord. A German officer escorted us out of the prison compound to a large meeting hall in Hammerstein. We had to give this up when the Russian army came through Poland. We marched westward to escape the Russians and were liberated by the American army after marching for 52 days and 500 miles on a ration of one or two potatoes each night. I carried my Bible in my backpack and my New Testament in my left shirt pocket. How I survived, only the Lord knows.

F. Paul Dallas
WWII • ETO
Past National Commander
American Ex-POW Association 2003-2004

My advice for life is to never give up; you will never succeed at much if you give up. Make an effort to always do what is right. Your character and your integrity depend on making the right choices in life. As far as faith, I would encourage you to trust in God. We read in Proverbs 3:5-6, "Trust in the Lord with all thine heart; and lean not unto thine own understanding. In all thy ways acknowledge Him and He shall direct thy paths."

HE WAS AND HE IS MY STRENGTH

I grew up on a farm deep in the Mississippi farm country. We were a large family of eight children. Our mother and father taught us the importance of God, country, and family. I would not have survived the horrors of WWII without God by my side and the strong desire to be reunited with my loved ones. He was my strength during the time I spent as a prisoner of war in a forced labor camp. It was the coldest winter in Europe in 50 years. We were beaten, starved, and forced to work in weather below zero. Some of my fellow POWs froze to death; others starved to death. My strength in God and my determination are what brought me back home.

Always have an abiding faith in God and be determined in all your endeavors, remember freedom is not free, ask any ex-POW. I hope our future generations will remember we fought for their freedom. To ensure the security of our nation we must always maintain a strong military.

Colonel George "Bud" Day
U.S. Air Force (Ret.) • Vietnam
Medal of Honor

Everyone needs a role model, an individual who will make you a better person and a better citizen. Perhaps the best role model would be Jesus Christ. He taught us to lead by teaching us how to follow. God gave us standards to live by, called the Ten Commandments. When asked what is the greatest commandment, Jesus said to love God and love your neighbor as yourself. Living out these standards will never put you on the wrong side of any problem.

My advice for life is: Have faith in God, trust in Him, and encourage your children and grandchildren to do the same!

CITATION

On 26 August 1967, Col. Day was forced to eject from his aircraft over North Vietnam when it was hit by ground fire. His right arm was broken in 3 places, and his left knee was badly sprained. He was immediately captured by hostile forces and taken to a prison camp where he was interrogated and severely tortured. After causing the guards to relax their vigilance, Col. Day escaped into the jungle and began the trek toward South Vietnam. Despite injuries inflicted by fragments of a bomb or rocket, he continued southward surviving only on a few berries and uncooked frogs. He successfully evaded enemy patrols and reached the Ben Hai River, where he encountered U.S. artillery barrages. With the aid of a bamboo log float, Col. Day swam across the river and entered the demilitarized zone. Due to delirium, he lost his sense of direction and wandered aimlessly for several days.

After several unsuccessful attempts to signal U.S. aircraft, he was ambushed and recaptured by the Viet Cong, sustaining gunshot wounds to his left hand and thigh. He was returned to the prison from which he had escaped and later was moved to Hanoi after giving his captors false information to questions put before him. Physically, Col. Day was totally debilitated and unable to perform even the simplest task for himself. Despite his many injuries, he continued to offer maximum resistance. His personal bravery in the face of deadly enemy pressure was significant in saving the lives of fellow aviators who were still flying against the enemy.

Col. Day's conspicuous gallantry and intrepidity at the risk of his life above and beyond the call of duty are in keeping with the highest traditions of the U.S. Air Force and reflect great credit upon himself and the U.S. Armed Forces.

Irving Day
WWII • ETO

My advice for life is: Have a faith in God, trust in Him, and encourage your children and your grandchildren to do the same.

HIS KINDNESS

I must have missed the lecture on "Bail-out Procedure." On April 11, 1944, I found myself confronted with the necessity of leaving my burning B-24 Liberator bomber, which had been critically damaged by flak over Germany. I was convinced that I could not leave through the small, nose-wheel hatch. After some vacillation, I decided that my bride would want me to at least try to exit. I stood beside that hole in the floor, hesitating; the next thing I knew I was falling in space. To this day, I am convinced it was the hand of God that pushed me out of that airplane. It had to be Him as Marin was definitely not present to assist me, only the thought of her! I discovered later that I bumped my head as I fell, a persistent trauma, but small cost for my life.

When an airplane was shot down over enemy territory prior to D-Day, it became a foregone conclusion that the occupants were destined to be either POW or KIA. To this day, I still do not know why I was spared, but I thank God daily for His kindness in allowing me to become a prisoner of war (and, more importantly, an ex-POW)! I do not brag that God protected me, but I am completely mystified.

The loss of one's freedom, devastating though it may seem at the time, is a temporary condition. However, the punishment of incarceration without crime for just doing one's duty is for most individuals a psyche-scarring experience. It is difficult for such subjects to provide leadership or respond to leadership of their peers. The ex-POW is prone to consider his cup to be half-empty, instead of still half-full. He dwells upon reasons why a project might fail, whereas a non-POW would consider reasons for success.

Whether he recognizes these truths or not, the ex-POW needs God's help and the reassurance of God's love, even though that love has already been demonstrated through His great gift of life. By admitting our frailty and striving with prayer to rise above it, we can hope to inspire our children and grandchildren to respect us and to frequently rely on God in their lives.

Rear Admiral Jeremiah Denton
U.S. Navy (Ret.) • Vietnam

My creed for life is the Apostles' Creed. My code of conduct is derived from the Ten Commandments and Jesus' command to "love God, and love your neighbor as you love yourself." As an American naval officer, I derived motivation to serve my nation because of my love for my country. I also believe that Americans have a special justification to love their country derived from a love of God. America was founded as "one nation under God." Our founding fathers deliberately based their experiment in democracy upon the premise that the compassion and the self-discipline required for the success of a democracy can only come from citizens who believe strongly in God.

Due to our nation's founding premise, I found it easy to serve in a profession that protected our land. My generation helped to protect and ensure the survival of our nation against Fascism and Soviet Communism. Now our greatest enemy is the threat that would do away with America's belief in the founding premise, its founding thesis.

If we continue to increase our forgetfulness of God's ultimate significance, then America will not survive. I strive for the ultimate significant success—heaven—by loving and serving God, country, and family.

THE SACRED HEART OF JESUS

To those who are non-Catholics among the readers, let me preface my story with an explanation of the Roman Catholic devotion to "The Sacred Heart of Jesus." Jesus, of course, has both a human and divine nature and took on a human body, and all the natural characteristics of a human when He was on earth. His brain and sensory system enabled Him to think and feel as a human being. His divine nature rendered Him a sinless soul but He felt the temptations of a human being, and all the physical pains, pleasures, sights, and emotions of a human being. Thus the immensity of His suffering for our salvation is more palpably understood and appreciated by us. It is a Catholic tradition to regard His heart as the center, the symbol of His own humanity, the "source" of His human compassion and His love as He felt it and showed it on earth.

The love resulting in the miracle of Cana is one example of what could be attributed to His Sacred Heart. We feel we can "get to Him" better, if you will, by appealing to that copiously loving heart. I had adopted that devotion and frequently uttered the prayer, "Sacred Heart of Jesus, I place my trust in Thee," which was the standard prayer of that devotion. I said it frequently, at least every night in prison.

Okay, with that said, let's go back to 1967, about two years after I was shot down. Those years were probably the worst in terms of suffering for me. For a considerable portion of that time I had served as senior officer for all the American POWs, responsible for issuing orders defining specific lines of resistance on unexpected challenges which arose, representing our complaints about out treatment to our captors, and generally feeling responsible for our morale and performance of duty. Simply being a POW involved plenty of stress, along with long periods of physical and mental suffering. But for those finding themselves senior over an isolated group of POWs, there was extra pressure.

The context of the timeframe of the incident I am about to relate was in the middle of the four years of intense mistreatment: mid 1967. Robbie Risner, then I, then Jim Stockdale had served as Senior Ranking Officer, (SRO), in that sequence since October 1965 when the torture began. At this particular point in time, they were both isolated, and I was trying to act as SRO again in a camp called "Las Vegas" where most of the POWs were being kept. Vegas was like a hotel with fairly small cells, most of them were sharing common walls with one or two other cells.

57

Many of us had been moved to Vegas from the "Zoo" where there were separate buildings, perhaps eight, holding a total of upwards of 100 prisoners. This arrangement permitted the North Vietnamese to erect bamboo walls cutting off visual contact between the buildings, which greatly impeded our audio contact because the walls limited maximum range of sound. The guards could use the walls to hide behind and catch people in one building trying to communicate with one another. Torture was always bestowed on POWs caught communicating, along with other unpleasant measures intended to intimidate the man from communicating in the future. This rendered communications difficult compared to the Vegas situation. We had been doing pretty well with tapping on the walls at Vegas for a number of months, but then the purge came that caused Stockdale's temporary isolation, and I inherited the sack.

To inhibit and virtually prevent me from communicating as SRO, they stationed a guard in a chair at the door of my cell. At all times, his chair was leaned back against the door, and the back of his head rested against the door. The acoustics were such that he could easily hear any tap, no matter how soft. Communications and prayer were by far the biggest factors supporting our morale and performance of duty.

At that time morale was low for three reasons: First, for a number of months, torture was being applied more intensely because the war was being intensified. The enemy was in an ugly mood, and we knew prisoners were being promptly and severely tortured. We could hear their screams from a distance in another part of the prison complex. A purge among those POWs who had been in captivity longer was underway in an effort to break our chain of command and destroy our will to resist. Second, the news about the war which we were receiving made it evident that it was extremely unlikely the POWs would be released in any reasonable or early timeframe, and the conclusions that we would never be released were floating around in our minds. Third, communication was almost nil.

I was intensely frustrated and chagrined at my lack of ability to communicate. Though I would have never admitted it, I was also of the belief that the U.S. was beginning to experience a growing anti-war movement. This sentiment would not likely improve our victory chances or any escalation of the scope and intensity of the U.S. offensive campaign, which many of us felt was necessary. Less importantly but of considerable effect on us, the end of the war did indeed seem further away, and release less certain. The screams of the prisoners in torture did not help my morale.

During this phase I was enjoying the company of Jim Mulligan, my occasional cellmate. At this point in time, Jim was sleeping in the upper bunk. It was midday, siesta time, and the screams occasionally broke the normal silence for that time of day. I was praying, as usual, that God's will be done, but that I hoped His will would include, among other things, improving our present situation because I was in leg irons and a guard was looking right at me. I prayed especially that He would let me come up with a means of communications that could be effectively used even when I was unable to move. Finally, as my last prayer, with special earnestness, I uttered the words, "Sacred Heart of Jesus, I place my trust in Thee."

In only a few seconds, I clearly heard an incredibly kind, dignified, but commanding voice, which I took to be the voice of Jesus Himself. The voice said clearly and rather slowly, "Say, Sacred Heart of Jesus, I give myself to You." I was almost knocked down with a wave of awe upon hearing the voice. It was the most real and the most amazing thing that ever happened to me. The speaker of those words, of course, was not only assuring me of having heard my prayer, but had instructed me to deliver it in the future with new wording and meaning. I was not to say I merely trusted Him, but transcending that, I was to GIVE MYSELF, (all of me, all of my concerns) not just to THEE, as to a formal, omnipotent other type of supreme being, but to give myself to YOU, the familiar designation of a friend or a brother. And the tone and inflection of the voice conveyed the same mood of brotherly familiarity and assurance.

It may sound kooky, but I know it happened, and I know it was real, more than I know my name is what it is, or that my wife is really my wife. For what it is worth, I can assure you that for me the prayer has worked. A few months later at a camp called Alcatraz where eleven of us were isolated for over two years, I did have a brainstorm which permitted me to devise the reliable, undetectable communications method for which I had specifically prayed. In many other painful situations, the prayer has since brought relief to me and to others who used it after I confided to them about the prayer.

C. Earl Derrington
WWII • ETO
Past National Commander
American Ex-POW Association, 1983-1984

Every facet of one's life is molded by the events encountered along the way. My formative years began with a loving mother, father, and brother. Church was a very important issue in my family. Consequently, when I became a POW in Germany in 1944, it was my faith and the strong bond of love within my family that sustained me.

As an adult, I find that the more I give of my time and of myself in helping others, the more enriched my life becomes. My advice for young people of today is to preserve the family, strengthen their spiritual faith, and keep their commitment to God, family, and country.

IT'S PAYBACK TIME

I entered the Army in June 1943 and was assigned to Company E of the 310th Infantry, the 78th Division. On December 13, I was wounded by a mortar burst and sustained numerous deep shrapnel wounds to my leg, back, near my spine, and my shoulder. One day later I was captured. Initially, I was a prisoner at Stalag VIG, but the camp was bombed, so we were forced to march across the Rhine to Stalag XIIA. I had not recovered from the wounds, and they became infected. An Army physician had to operate and remove the shrapnel fragments without an anesthetic. He believed that I would probably not survive without surgery and said I might not even survive with it. Conditions were primitive and there were no medications for pain or for the infection. After the surgery, my physical condition progressively deteriorated.

Before the march to Stalag XII, we were each given a ration of bread. My friend had his ration stolen so he had no food for the march. During the march I grew weaker and was unable to eat, so I offered him my bread. He refused, saying, "I won't take your bread." He knew that I also needed food to survive, but after two days, he said, "I will take some of your bread, but I am going to pay you back!"

When we reached the new camp, my friend was befriended by a German guard who was a sergeant. One day the German gave my friend some bread, cheese, and jelly. Late at night I heard someone move near where I was sleeping. I couldn't see who it was because the room was totally black. It was Arthur Rubenstein, my friend. He leaned down and whispered in my ear, "It's payback time," and he gave me the food.

Over time I continued to get sicker, grew weaker, and was moved to the prison hospital. It was a hospital in name only. There was no treatment and no medicine. Due to a high fever I was unconscious for one month. When Arthur came to visit, he pleaded with the Germans to do something, but was told that "nothing could be done." He convinced other prisoners to help him collect snow to pack around my infected leg in an attempt to break the fever. I survived because my friend and other prisoners cared. I can still hear his words today, "It's payback time." Always remember to appreciate your friends!

Colonel David Eberly
U.S. Air Force (Ret.) • Persian Gulf War

"Good morning, Lord; and Lord, it is a good morning." These words of Chaplain Leon Hill helped me start each day during my 43 days in Saddam's prisons. They represent the power of positive thinking and the foundation of Christian faith. Locked away where daylight and darkness seem to be just another part of an endless nightmare, time is measured in moments; some moments are a lifetime. Nothing was done on schedule, and my own worst enemy was self-pity, anxiety, and impatience. Living had taken on a whole new meaning.

When faith falters, life's challenges often prompt us to ask, "Why me, Lord?" Yet we cannot know or even imagine the opportunities that God gives us. Christian faith is based on an acceptance of His promise to care for us throughout eternity. In troubled times, when life is defined by the moment, we must trust His grace and draw on our faith to find the inner strength and courage to face our deepest fears or to overcome the most challenging tragedies. We must simply have faith.

Faith is knowing you are not alone.
It is believing His promise, and it is living His word.
It is having the courage to stand for Him
And having the will to speak with Him.
Faith is calling His name when we face the unknown
It is knowing His way.
It is comfort, it is peace, and in this trust, He is.

ARE YOU CHRISTMAS?

In our toughest times, our Shepherd is always on guard. Such was the occasion during my experience (as detailed in my book *Faith Beyond Belief*) in the 1991 war with Iraq. After being shot down, I was captured on the Syrian border. Then, on the road to Baghdad, I met a most unusual man who reinforced God's promise to "care for a fallen sparrow."

Near the Iraq/Syria border, we were pushed into the back of a white Toyota. We lost all bearings as we zoomed along. Jumping from the car would be foolish. Besides, there was no way Grif (my backseater) could get out of the middle seat. We had to sit and keep our senses keen.

Arriving in a blacked-out Baghdad, we turned off a boulevard and hooked back left and parked the car. Once out of the car, we were pushed along a narrow walkway bounded by tall evergreens that led to a small white house. The driver's knock on the door reflected his weariness and growing frustration. The agitated tone of the Arabic greeting from the man at the door signaled that we were not welcome and this would be just another stop to survive on our journey. Here, instead of another interrogation, however, we would be exposed to a most unusual enemy soldier.

In the dim candlelight we could see the entry hall with stairs on our right leading up to the second floor. Grif and I were made to sit side by side on the fourth row of steps. The doors to the other rooms were closed, but we had gotten a glimpse of several men sitting around a heater who were arguing loudly, and it seemed as though they were cursing our driver for bringing us there.

We were being guarded by two Iraqis: one had an automatic rifle, the other brandished a knife. One seemed more intent on jabbing at us. Silently, I continued to pray for strength. He ripped Grif's T-shirt over his head and threatened us with his knife, which drew a rebuke from the other man. Now we were alone with the armed guard standing at the foot of the stairs facing us. After some time, with muffled talk in the background, he leaned forward and asked us quietly, "Are you Christmas?"

"Christmas?" I said, puzzled. "He must mean Christian," Grif whispered. Although my mind filled instantly with the fear that our Arab guard might simply be looking for a reason to kill us, I also felt that God was with us now as always. "Yes," I responded. "Me too," said the guard. How ironic that here, along this seemingly endless, dismal road, we would meet a man with such courage. Our Shepherd was on guard.

Carl Edwards
WWII • ETO

Following the orders of my Commanding Officer, I laid down my weapon and surrendered to the enemy in WWII. While it is important to lead, it is equally important to follow a command. That is the only reason I am alive today.

When God gives an order from His Word, it is in our best interest to follow that order. When we surrender to the enemy, we give up all our earthly freedoms, but he cannot take away our faith in God.

My code of conduct is read God's Word, pray for knowledge, then, with humility, apply these to your daily walk.

A REFLECTION OF GOD'S LOVE

After being captured in Belgium during the Battle of the Bulge on December 22, 1944, I was in Stalag IVB. From there I was moved to Stalag VIIIA at Gorlitz Germany. We were forced to leave Gorlitz on February 14, 1945, and we marched to Ditford, Germany. On April 12, 1945, we were liberated by U.S. forces.

The march from the front lines until our liberation was more than 600 miles. I was surprised to learn that even in war some of the German people were still willing to help us. On many occasions during this march, women would come to the POWs and give them food. The food was usually bread and boiled potatoes. There were many other acts of kindness, but the one I remember most vividly happened to me on the day we were liberated (which also happened to be the day that President Roosevelt died). An elderly man approached me as I was walking in the small town. In broken English, he invited me into his home. As I followed him inside, his wife was preparing breakfast, which consisted of black bread, molasses, goat's milk, and coffee.

The lady had hand clippers and offered to cut my long hair, and she then offered me a razor to shave my beard. She showed me her family pictures, explaining that two of their sons had been lost in the war. After feeding me and allowing me to clean up in their home, she told me I could lay down on the couch and sleep.

Deep into my nap, I was awakened by a loud argument. Two young Germans had entered the home of the elderly couple and said that they were going to take me outside and kill me. The elderly couple pleaded with the two young men. After a heated argument, the men left. The lady would not let me leave the home until she was sure that the young men were gone.

It was this humane treatment that made me realize there are people in the world, no matter what loss they have experienced themselves, that are still willing to help others in need. This demonstration of kindness can only come from God. Oh, how great is the love of God shown by acts of kindness!

In the Sermon on the Mount, we were commanded to even love our enemies. I believe this German couple's demonstration of love toward me is a reflection of the love of God. In John 3:16 we read, "For God so loved the world that He gave His only begotten Son that whosoever believeth in him shall have everlasting life." Thank God!

Colonel Lee Ellis
U.S. Air Force (Ret.) • Vietnam

As a POW I tried to live by the American Fighting Man's Code of Conduct. In the process I learned many things that have helped me in my struggle to live a life that honors God and blesses my fellow man.

1. Live by principles and values. The Bible offers truths that have stood the test of time and can guide you in relationships, finances, business, and literally every area of your life.

2. Have the courage (faith) to do what is right even when it is difficult or unpopular. It's the price of integrity, and our senior officers paid it through their personal sacrifice.

3. Be yourself. You are a unique creation so don't compare yourself to someone else. Focus on your talents and passions and use them to accomplish your life purpose/mission.

4. Think about the long-term goal and beware of taking the easy way out. My five and a half years in the camps taught me the value of commitment and persistence.

5. Take care of your people. Avoid the natural urge to further your own self interest at the expense of others: Be a giver, not a taker.

6. Face up to your weaknesses and learn about your blind spots. In the camps, we had lots of time to take inventory and get feedback. When you admit you don't have it all together, God can do a great work in your life.

WE HAVE A FRIEND IN JESUS

No one plans to be a POW, but in many ways we were well-prepared for the experience in North Vietnam. Our military training and discipline were crucial and highlighted the importance of training and development for success in any field. We were also blessed with a reservoir of experienced, courageous leaders who guided us through those difficult times. They set the example, took the heat, and kept us united and focused on a common goal—return with honor.

The greatest blessing was the faith that my family had given me. I grew up in a Christian home where we went to church every Sunday and read the Bible regularly. While I was still young, their faith became my faith, and my relationship with the Lord sustained me in difficult times. Likewise, the prayers of my family and many others came right through those prison walls and were a great inspiration. Whether in a POW camp or facing the struggles and successes of everyday life, I know that we have a Friend in Jesus who loves us and wants the best for us. It doesn't get any better than that. Proverbs 3:5-6 says, "Trust in the Lord with all your heart and lean not on your own understanding; in all your ways acknowledge him, and he will make your paths straight."

Wendell Fetters
WWII • ETO

I learned at a very early age that I had to pay for my actions, especially those that were bad. My father would make me go down to the creek and cut my own switch. I would walk around for quite awhile hoping my father might forget about my punishment. He never did! I learned that a willow switch was so thin that it would leave a welt on my bottom, but a larger switch left a bruise. Being forced to cut my own switch taught me a valuable lesson that helped me behave. As a POW, I learned another valuable lesson—freedom is not free! You are at the mercy of your captors. You were not given the opportunity to cut your own switch. You were absolutely helpless and had to follow every order.

My motto for life is: Always be honest; your word is your bond. When you tell the truth, you will never have to try and remember what you said. My spiritual advice would be put God first, then country, and both above self.

HE IS ALWAYS PRESENT

On December 23, 1944, we were shot down during the Battle of the Bulge. We were scheduled to be sent to Barth, which originally was a POW camp for Air Force officers. Later in the war, it was for non-commissioned officers as well.

When our train, which contained 50-60 Army Air Force personnel, was shot up in the rail yards of Berlin, we were dumped off at Stalag IIIA at Luckenwald, Germany. It was a pretty dismal place. We all had lice, bedbugs, and sand fleas for company.

The British compound was to the west; the Russian compound to the east. We were not fed well, but the Russians, it appeared, were fed even less. The problem, the Germans told us, was that our Red Cross parcels came out of Switzerland, and our Air Force had bombed all the rail yards and bridges, and shot up the trucks on the roads so no parcels got through to the POWs. That was probably true, but as a result, we were fed a slice of what we referred to as "sawdust" black bread, one or two small potatoes a day, and sometimes a cup of soup with questionable ingredients.

Our rations, like the Russians, were based on the daily head count because food was so important. During the daily head count, the Russians would hold up their dead as long as it was possible just to get their extra rations. It sounds gruesome, but for survival it was extremely important.

When we were liberated by the Russian Army, it was a joyful occasion. Everyone was happy, and the fences were torn down so all the prisoners could intermingle. A Russian, probably an officer, who was wearing brown trousers with a red stripe down the leg, took me by the arm and steered me into the nearest barracks. It was dark, dank, and bug-infested. At the north end of the building in all its glory, was a beautiful statue of Jesus in a garden-like setting. It was complete with angels painted in the background. I could hardly believe my eyes! I was awestruck. Here in the midst of squalor and despair was the work of what we had been led to believe were godless Russians. It proved to me that even in Communism, Christ was ever present!

Steve Fitzgerald
WWII • ETO

Always trust in and obey God. At times life can be difficult and even seem unfair. No matter what the situation, always remember to pray and to thank Him for what He has done, what He is doing, and what He will do in your life.

In Romans 5:2-5 we read, "And we rejoice in the hope of the glory of God. Not only so, but we also rejoice in our sufferings, because we know that suffering produces perseverance; perseverance, character; and character hope. And hope does not disappoint."

THE POWER OF PRAYER

The following is what impelled me, through my life, to distinguish between success and the appreciation of the significance of Jesus Christ.

I attended a rather strict ROTC military high school where I won some academic awards and a medal for excellence in military science and tactics. Looking back, I believe I was an arrogant, self-confident know-it-all until I came very close to dying from a ruptured appendix during a field maneuver far from a hospital.

Graduating from high school in 1944 at age 18, I volunteered for immediate induction into the army infantry, the "Queen of Battle." I had hoped to go to Officer Candidate School and, after combat, apply for language school to enter into military intelligence training. However, the Battle of the Bulge broke out in Europe in December 1944, and we were taken out of incomplete basic training with orders to go to Europe. I was given a two-day "Delay in Route" to spend time at home on Christmas Eve and Christmas Day. Being at boot camp was a relief in a sense because my beloved mother, an Irish Catholic of the old school, insisted on obeying not only the Ten Commandments but every rule and regulation of the church. She insisted on attending Mass on Christmas Day even though I told her I had a lot of sleep to catch up on. Before I left, she gave me a gift of long underwear. She had sewn the picture of Jesus on the chest over my heart. I thought to myself, "I guess I have to accept this gift but I will never wear this!"

A month or so later I was captured and forced to march across freezing central Europe with very little to eat, sleeping mostly in the open. Carrying our sick and wounded was another major burden. One of my feet became infected and so swollen that it was twice its normal size. Surgery and possible amputation was to be done on my foot for which there was no anesthetic. Looking around the room, I realized that if I survived the surgery, I would most likely die from an infection. While being held down on a dirty mattress in a filthy prison camp infirmary by five men, I could only move my head. I began to pray as hard as I could, I looked down, and I saw the little cloth picture of Jesus that my mother had sewn on my long underwear over my heart. I was praying very earnestly that I would not lose my foot. The American doctor, a paratrooper, told me that he would not amputate but he was not at all sure that he could save the foot. I knew the Lord Jesus Christ could. Following that prayer I had complete and total peace. To this day, my feet are perfect, and I enjoy good health.

William Fornes
Korea

I think the best advice anyone has given about becoming a POW is the advice of Congressman Sam Johnson in the video, *ECHOS OF CAPTIVITY*—"Don't get captured."

After I retired from the military, I volunteered for seven years teaching the code of conduct for the Airman Leadership course at Moody Air Force Base. I frequently speak to ROTC and JROTC units. If I were to give advice about my creed or code of conduct for life, this comes to mind: I believe our nation needs to get its priorities in line, not only the military but in our society as a whole. For years we fought the cold war, the war on drugs and the war on terrorism. I see the American public as self-serving and without resolve. As a result, we are undermining the principles our forefathers defended for us and expected us to preserve.

RETURN TO THE FORTRESS

When the Korean War started, we were operating with leftover WWII technology, equipment and principles. Our mindset was win the war, and, if captured, then give only your name, rank, service number and date of birth. But it was a new kind of war conducted by the United Nations with 17 nations. The war probably lasted two years longer because of the POWs held by both North and South Korea.

After Korea came Vietnam, a very costly effort that affected the military more than we realize. We won the Gulf War in 1991, but we are still there 15 years later. Then it was Grenada, Haiti, Bosnia, Kosovo, Afghanistan, and now Iraqi Freedom. Where do we go next?

We give our military an objective but always with extreme limitations. Don't tie the hands of those who would protect our freedom! I am reminded of the verse of scripture engraved on the prisoner of war statue in Georgia, "Return to your fortress, O prisoners of hope" (Zechariah 9:12). That's what we need to do. We need to return once again to those principles and values that made America great.

William Foster
WWII • ETO

Always stand up for what you believe in, no matter the consequence. Live life to the fullest. Make the most of every day. Live by the Golden Rule: do for others what you would like to have them do for you.

—•••—

OH, GOD...DON'T LET IT CARTWHEEL

On the morning of December 23, 1944, when I opened the throttle of my P-47 Thunderbolt heading down the runway, I had a feeling that "this was it." My squadron, the 378th, flew out of a forward airstrip near Etain, France. It was my 13th mission. As I began climbing away from the runway, I tried to shake off the concern, attributing the feeling to 13th mission jitters. We were accompanying C-47 cargo planes as they dropped badly needed supplies to General McAuliffe's besieged troops at Bastogne. After escorting the C-47s to Bastogne, the C-47s turned back and headed toward the coast.

The fighters remained and began looking for targets of opportunity. I was one of four fighters directed to attack German positions at Hill 507. There were several German tanks in fortified positions there, firing at American positions. As we began the attack, suddenly things went very wrong. We began to receive a lot of 20-millimeter fire, and the huge four-bladed propeller of the Thunderbolt was hit. Severe vibrations shook the aircraft so violently that I was afraid of the possibility of complete structural failure. The instrument panel of the fighter was jumping up and down as I began to lose altitude. Initially I thought I might be able to make it back, but I continued to lose altitude and as I was nearing 300 feet, the situation continued to deteriorate rapidly. It was obvious that both time and good luck had run out simultaneously.

I spotted a small patch of open ground that appeared to be about five acres. Lining the plane up as well as possible, I prepared to belly land the crippled ship. I opened the canopy so it wouldn't jam as I shut off all the switches and the fuel. I absolutely didn't want a fire. I was never an overly religious person, but with the impact I shouted a spontaneous prayer: "Oh God! Don't let it cartwheel!"

I knew that if one of the wings hit the ground, the plane would cartwheel over and over, and my chance of survival would be markedly decreased. When the plane hit, it slithered along the snow-covered ground in an upright position. I believe my shouted spontaneous prayer was heard. The huge, radial engine separated from its mounting and rolled beneath the airplane, and one wing was sheared off by a tree. As the ship disintegrated around me, it finally slid to a stop. I quickly unstrapped myself, climbed out of the wreckage, and ran for some bushes.

The ground was snow-covered and the Germans had little difficulty in tracking me to where I was trying to hide. Initially I was moved to what appeared to be a small farmhouse, which turned out to be a crossroads café. Later that night I was moved toward the rear. Walking along the snow-covered road in the moonlight, I was surprised at the beauty in such a bad situation. The bad situation, however, quickly turned worse because we suddenly started taking artillery fire from our own guys. Some of it was really close. Everybody ran for the ditch beside the road. I felt pain in my backside but figured that a piece of rock had hit me. Initially it felt like I had been hit by a hammer, but then the pain seemed to go away, followed by numbness. When the shelling finally stopped, I stood and realized my foot felt warm. Checking my boot, I realized it was full of blood. I thought, "I survived the crash only to be wounded by my comrades miles away." I was hospitalized for awhile due to the wound.

I eventually ended up in Stalag Luft I near Barth, Germany. On April 30, 1945, the German guards fled due to the advancing Russian troops. We were transferred to American control and flown by B-17 bombers to France and eventually back home.

Carl Fyler
WWII • ETO

During the war, I always accompanied my crew to the base Protestant chapel for services. In combat when a flak battery got a bead on my ship, I'd pray that I could get my crew back to England. Sometimes the whole sky was full of flak. Once two big shells tore up the right wing, killing two engines, and the plane fell 21,000 feet. With the help of my co-pilot, we tipped the B-17 over on the left wing and flew sideways for 500 miles at 100 feet. We destroyed two enemy planes sent out to get us and landed at an emergency field in England.

At the VA when asked if I believe in God, I answer, "Yes." So much has happened to me; God must have saved me for a reason.

UNCOMMON VALOR A COMMON VIRTUE

At 0200 hours, November 29, 1943, the officer of the day (OD) woke me and said, "You're flying today!" I replied, "No, I'm convalescing from being run down by the squadron jeep!" The OD insisted, so I dressed and headed to headquarters in the dark. Sure enough, my name was on the list to lead the high squadron. I hurried through breakfast, gathered my combat gear, and headed out to the plane assigned to me, a B-17 named the Dark Horse.

This mission was my 25th, and I was so battle weary that I could hardly function. Maybe subconsciously I felt it would soon be over, one way or the other. This day as we approached the target, there were only two of us left in the high squadron.

As we dropped our bombs on the target, the flak hit us both. Lieutenant Bob Ward, my co-pilot, was wounded in the face. The next burst hit the tail section, and the plane lurched violently. Both waist gunners were thrown against the roof and slammed to the floor, which was littered ankle-deep in empty shell casings.

The two engines on the right were damaged by flak. Bob shut them down and feathered the props. I was not aware that the right stabilizer and part of the right wing were gone. Moments later another engine caught fire, and I was flying on only one engine on the left wing. I had to put both feet on the control column to hold the nose down. I knew that we were in deep trouble because I could not steer or fly the plane to the west and home.

We were then attacked by FW 190s. One was firing as he passed our left wing tip and was so close that I thought he had hit us. S/Sgt. Bill Anderson, the top turret gunner, was hit in the thigh by a 20-mm shell. He was knocked out of the turret onto the flight deck. Other shells had passed through the cockpit, and the navigator and I were also hit. I could feel blood running down my back and pooling in the seat. Having lost all radio communication, I did not know the condition of the rest of the crew. I motioned to Bob and Bill to get out, and they exited the aircraft through open bomb bay doors.

I continued to try to fly west without success. By now the ship was in a downward spiral to the right, and I could see things on the ground rotating. I realized that the situation was hopeless and that it was time for me to go! I crawled under the floor of the aircraft to make sure the men had gotten out. They were gone and so was the door to the hatch, so I dropped through the opening and slid along the plane. When I was behind the plane I reached for the ripcord but had difficulty finding it. Groping with both hands, I finally located it and pulled. Nothing happened. I pulled again, harder this time. A small chute appeared and then the main canopy opened. As I hung there, one of the FW190s made a pass at me, then another pass. I tried to swing back and forth by pulling on the risers. When I looked up, I realized that he had split the canopy of my chute, and I was falling too fast.

That is the last thing I remembered until I awoke on a pile of tree limbs. Looking up at a 60-foot pine tree, I realized that I had taken all the limbs off one side of the tree as I fell. Hitting the tree had probably saved me. It wasn't long before I was captured and taken to the small village of Delmenhorst. I was placed in a room with my wounded co-pilot, Bob Ward. Later I was moved by a pickup truck with a covered bed to a darkened concrete room, much like an underground dungeon. From there I was moved by train to the Dulag Luft interrogation center at Oberursel, a few miles from Frankfurt, from Frankfurt to Berlin, and then to Stalag Luft I near the city of Barth.

One dark, cold rainy day some other Americans were brought into the camp. I recognized one of them as my top turret gunner, S/Sgt Bill Addison. Up to that point I had only been able to account for three of my eleven-man crew. It was my first opportunity to find out about the rest of my crew. His news was not good, however. Bill had learned the rest of the story from the two waist gunners.

Our tail gunner was a soft-spoken, Polish-American boy, named Joe Sawicki. He had been awarded the Polish Royal Air Force Cross of Honor as well as the Polish Legion of Merit while flying with the RAF before he was assigned to our crew. Shortly after we had dropped our bombs on that last mission, Sawicki's arm had been severed below the elbow, and he had also sustained mortal wounds to his mid-section by the flak burst that struck the tail of the plane. Reasoning that he could not continue firing his twin .50 caliber guns with only one hand, he crawled forward to assist others. He found that the right waist gunner had a fractured arm and was also shot in the face. The left waist gunner had been hit in the forehead by fragments from one of the shells, and he also had a fractured arm. The ball turret gunner had been killed by machine gun fire. Sawicki helped both waist gunners get into their parachutes. He used his foot to kick out the door and wrestled both gunners to the exit, literally booting them out of the falling aircraft, thus saving their lives. All gave some, some gave all...Sawicki never made it out of the plane.

UNIFORM CODE OF CONDUCT

Article I: I am an American, fighting in the forces which guard my country and our way of life. I am prepared to give my life in their defense.

Article II: I will never surrender of my own free will. If in command, I will never surrender my men while they still have the means to resist.

Article III: If I am captured, I will continue to resist by all means available. I will make every effort to escape and aid others to escape. I will accept neither parole nor special favors from the enemy.

Article IV: If I become a prisoner of war, I will keep faith with my fellow prisoners. I will give no information nor take part in any action which might be harmful to my comrades. If I am senior, I will take command. If not, I will obey the lawful orders of those appointed over me and will back them up in every way.

Article V: When questioned, should I become a prisoner of war, I am bound to give only rank, service number, and date of birth. I will evade answering further questions to the utmost of my ability. I will make no oral or written statements disloyal to my country and its allies or harmful to their cause.

Article VI: I will never forget that I am an American, responsible for my actions, and dedicated to the principles which made my country free. I will trust in my God and in the United States of America.

Paul Galanti
Vietnam

The following is one of my favorite quotes—I close all my talks with it: "There's no such thing as a bad day when there's a doorknob on the inside of the door."

PROUD TO SERVE

As a cocky, young Navy pilot blasted from the sky over North Vietnam in my A-4 Skyhawk, I thought, "This can't be happening to me!" My next 2,432 days were spent in the various POW camps in North Vietnam, collectively called the Hanoi Hilton by its residents. It wasn't supposed to happen—but it did.

I really didn't expect to be held long. My estimate of release to the "Old Guys" upon arrival in Hanoi was six months to a year at most. The reason? I'd seen the plans for the total destruction of North Vietnam in 1965 but waited in vain for them to happen.

I spent more than a year in solitary confinement with the hours broken only by infrequent communications (tapping through 18 inches of concrete) with other Americans and a quarterly, miserable re-introduction to the "Camp Regulations for Captured American Criminals." I lived in ten camps scattered all over North Vietnam—several in Hanoi, the capital, a couple in the countryside including the Son Tay camp raided by U.S. Special Forces in November 1970, and one near Lang Son, a few kilometers from the Chinese border.

Despite all efforts to break the POWs, we remained as unified as was possible under the circumstances. The excellent leadership of Col. Robbie Risner and Cdr. James Stockdale, held us together under these difficult circumstances, and most of us came out better men than when we went in. We were proud to serve our country.

Len Gregg
WWII • ETO

"Always do what is right, this will gratify some people and will astonish the rest." These words, spoken many years ago by Mark Twain, are just as true today as they were then. Always doing right causes people to be at peace with themselves, and, even more importantly, to be at peace with God.

TRUST IN GOD

When the Japanese bombed Pearl Harbor in December 1941, I was a freshman in college in central Missouri at Warrensburg. In October 1942, I took the entrance examinations leading to the Army Air Force training to become a pilot and was called to active duty a few months later. Following numerous training assignments at many different locations and bases, I finally received my wings at Ellington Field, Texas, in Houston in June 1944.

Eager to get into the real action, I volunteered to fly combat duty. I was initially assigned as a co-pilot on a B-24 Liberator. For reasons unknown, we were ultimately assigned to the B-17 Flying Fortress rather that the B-24. Following a nine-week session of Operational Training at Dyersburg, Tennessee, we picked up our B-17 in Lincoln, Nebraska, and departed for overseas duty in October 1944. We assumed that we were heading to the 8th Air Force in England but were surprised when we opened our sealed orders to discover that we were assigned to Steparone as part of the 15th Air Force. Steparone was a base in Italy on the coast on the Adriatic Sea and also the home of the 483rd Bomb Group, and our squadron, the 480th.

Our first few weeks in Italy were spent in briefings and making flights to calibrate the equipment aboard the B-17. Inclement weather during mid-December kept the planes of our group grounded. Our first mission was Christmas Day, 1944; the destination was the oil refineries at Brux, Germany. During this mission we were flying in what was referred to as "the hole," which meant if the lead plane was hit, we would take over that position. The lead plane was, in fact, hit by flak, spiraled downward and became the only loss of the mission. We took over that position. We made it back to Steparone, realizing that we had survived our first baptism of fire.

On December 28th, our third mission, we were in the air at 7:00 a.m., headed for the railroad marshalling yards at Regensburg, Germany. We were again told to expect heavy flak from anti-aircraft guns. Not long after crossing the Alps, our formation was suddenly hit by approximately a dozen flak bursts. One of the bursts apparently knocked a hole in our number two engine, causing oil to spew back over the wing. As we attempted to feather the prop by turning the blades into the wind, our number three engine suddenly lost power. Dropping out of formation, further efforts to feather the prop proved unsuccessful. The prop, windmilling without oil, soon overheated the engine to the point of bursting into flames that streamed back over the wing.

The order to "abandon ship" was given over the intercom. I reached below my seat and grabbed the handle of my chest pack parachute, snapping its two buckles onto the two rings of the harness that we always wore while in flight. The chute, packed in a canvas bag one foot long and about six inches in diameter, looked very small and inadequate suspended on my chest. I hoped it would work.

After putting the plane on automatic pilot, I dropped to the passageway leading forward and crawled to the nose area. The bombardier and the navigator had already exited through a small door on the lower left side of the nose. I sat down, thrust my legs through a small opening, pulled down on the top of the framed opening to lighten my weight, and was promptly pulled out into the rushing air, just brushing past the flaming engine as I fell. After pulling the rip cord, I was thrilled to have the parachute deploy as designed. I looked back and could see the chutes of other crew members in the distance. As I descended, the chute began swaying back and forth and I landed not on my feet, but the back of my feet, then my backside, striking the back of my head. I was momentarily knocked unconscious. Regaining my senses, I saw a group of about 50 men, women, and children emerging from the timber and heading in my direction. When they reached me, I felt a great sense of relief to find that they were friendly, because it had been reported that downed airmen had sometimes been killed by hostile civilians.

One of the men in the group could speak some English, having spent two years in the States before the war. He served as an interpreter as we walked into a small dwelling in the village. I was given a glass of warm goat's milk to drink. After the first small sip, I was almost relieved when the interpreter ran in shouting that the Germans were coming. The two of us ran for the timber located about a hundred feet from the dwelling. As we entered the brush, I looked back to observe several motorcycles equipped with sidecars loaded with German soldiers. Although it was a close call, I was safe because the Germans apparently knew better than to follow us into the timber. The reason for their lack of enthusiasm became clear when, after walking a short distance, a uniformed soldier with a red star on his cap stepped from behind a tree with a rifle leveled toward us. I was now in the hands of the Yugoslav Partisans and would remain so for the next two weeks.

During that two week period, we moved from village to village, staying in small homes far behind enemy lines. One night around 10:00, wet and cold, we were let into a church that was cold and empty. There was a fireplace at the rear of the sanctuary, but no fuel was available. With the help of our guide, we sacrificed one of the wooden pews in order to keep from freezing and trusted that we were forgiven by the Lord for our action. When morning arrived, the fire had long since gone out, and our clothing was frozen to the stone floor.

In just a few more days we were moved to a building where almost 40 American airmen were already being held. Among them was an American sergeant with a two-way radio who was part of the underground pipeline that helped to rescue downed airmen. About an hour after we arrived, three C-47 transport planes swooped down into the meadow, taxied up to the building, and threw open the cargo doors. The engines were not even turned off. As the props kept turning, we loaded into the planes. The entire time to fill the planes must have taken only three or four minutes. We flew to Bari, Italy, and there we where questioned about our experiences and the conditions we left in Yugoslavia. That evening we flew back to Steparone and were flying missions again within a week. I guess the exuberance I felt returning back to Steparone would have been dampened had I known that nine missions and two months later, enemy flak would cause us to crash in the Yugoslav mountains and be taken as prisoners of war.

I have been asked after returning home if I had a faith during the rough times. My response has always been "Yes." Faith gives you the courage to make decisions when the chips are down, as well as the ability to leave the result to a higher authority. Only by trusting God is a person in a responsible position ever able to find peace.

Bruce Hall
WWII • ETO

I have tried to lead a life of helping others as a pharmacist, father, and leader with the American Ex-Prisoner of War Association. There is no greater calling than service to God, family, nation, and fellow man.

I WAS BLESSED

I was a private in the 45th Infantry Division, 157th Regiment during WWII. I joined them as a replacement just prior to landing at Salerno, Italy, on September 9, 1943, and was assigned to the heavy mortar platoon of Company H. My best buddy (Bob) was assigned to a rifle company at the same time. Two days later as we were advancing, I saw a GI get shot and fall. I managed to get him and pull him back to cover. When I turned him over, I discovered to my horror that it was Bob. He looked up at me, said my name, and died. To this day I wonder why I survived when he and so many others did not. I know I was not the only one who prayed, so why did I make it? I had determined that I would make it regardless of what happened, but I was blessed to be able to do so.

We advanced as far as the mountains at Cassino where the winter line of the German army stopped us. Our division was among those chosen to pull back to Naples to regroup for the landings at Anzio on January 19, 1944. I was there one month before being captured along with most of my battalion.

My entire life prior to going into the Army had been positive. Both my parents were active in church, as was I. I was also active in YMCA activities. It was this positive heritage that sustained me through the fierce fighting and my 15 months as a POW. I managed to escape in early April 1945. I weighed 98 pounds when I finally reached the American lines. The faith that had been instilled in me during my childhood enabled me to know that I could and would survive.

Commander Porter Halyburton
U.S. Navy (Ret.) • Vietnam

All through the seven and a half years of imprisonment in North Vietnam, my Christian faith was a constant source of great strength and comfort. I knew that this was something that my captors could never take away from me. Had they been able to destroy that faith, I do not think that I would have survived with any sense of integrity or honor. The struggle to live an honorable life and to find meaning in that life, no matter how miserable the circumstances, was the most important thing I could do.

Over time I developed what I refer to as a Life Statement. It is as follows: I wish, at the instant of my death, to be able to look back upon a full and fruitful Christian life, lived as an honest man who has constantly striven to improve himself and the world in which he lives, and to die forgiven by God, and have, with a clear conscience, the love and respect of my family and friends, and the peace of the Lord in my soul.

A WORSE PLACE

Two days after being shot down northwest of Hanoi in October 1965, I arrived at the Hoa Lo prison, the now-famous Hanoi Hilton. I was put in a small cell in an area that Americans called Heartbreak Hotel, and I was to find that this was a most appropriate name. Interrogations began immediately and increased in frequency and intensity. Every time I answered with "Name, Rank, Service Number and Date of Birth"—the only information permitted by the Code of Conduct.

After two weeks of threats, beatings, humiliations, and filthy conditions, the Rabbit (one of our guards) finally gave me an ultimatum in the form of a choice—to answer questions and move to a "nice camp" where I could be with my friends and enjoy good treatment and food, or to continue to refuse to cooperate and be moved to a much worse place where I would be alone and be punished for my bad attitude. Heartbreak was pretty grim—tiny cells with concrete bunks and built-in leg irons, so I could hardly imagine anything worse.

Actually the choice was pretty easy at this point. My prayers and the advice from other Americans in Heartbreak gave me strength and some confidence. There was nothing I couldn't live with. I did not believe there was a better place, and I was not going to give them anything in any case. So I chose the worse one. Sure enough, it was worse, but different. It was a larger cell in a building that had been named "The Office" in a prison called the "Zoo." The exterior was pleasant enough—it had been a film studio used by the propaganda branch of the army with stucco building and red tile roofs, a swimming pool in the center, and various kinds of trees. On the inside, the windows had all been barred and then bricked up on the inside to within three inches of the top. Since I had been moved in the middle of the night, the cell was completely dark and I had to feel my way around the walls to even know how big it was. The floor was covered in dust and smelled of wet concrete. This smell and the bleakness and the blackness of the cell got to me that night, and I felt some of the terror that Fortunato, Poe's character in the "The Cask of Amontillado," must have felt as he realized that he had been bricked up in the cellar. I longed for and prayed for something green, something alive, and something friendly.

One morning very early I heard a faint scraping at the window, almost an invitation to investigate. I jumped and grabbed the top bricks in the window and struggled up far enough to look over. And there, sticking through the slats of the shutter but beyond the bars, was a green leaf. It was the most beautiful leaf that I had ever seen, and I knew at once that God had instructed the tree outside to move its branch just enough to present me with this gift, this sign that I was not alone. The cell, as well as my spirits, brightened up considerably.

I also received another gift while I was there—a little extra food and a bit of humor. The turnkey appeared unexpectedly one day and gave me two pieces of paper and a small dish containing a little ball of rice. The papers contained the Camp Regulations, one in English and the other in Vietnamese. He pointed to the wall and then left. I thought, *This is pretty cool—something to read and a little snack.* When the guard returned, he was furious that I had eaten the "glue" and had not pasted the regulations on the wall as I was supposed to. He must have thought that I was the dumbest person on earth, and he dutifully showed me how to use the rice to stick the papers to the wall. At this point I decided that playing dumb was probably a good thing to do and would probably work.

Interrogations continued day after day. "Where you from? What kind of aircraft you fly? How many missions you fly?" And again, the same old threat—cooperate or you will move to a much worse place. Soon enough the threat became a reality, and I was awakened in the middle of the night and blindfolded. With my meager bedroll under one arm, I was led across the prison to the back side of a large building that I knew was called the "Auditorium."

My new home was a storage room in the back, up a few steps from the central room that had been used for larger groups to view films. It had no light but the window had not been bricked up, although it did have bars and tight-fitting shutters. Again I had to feel my way around the cell in the dark and found that it was quite small. I tapped on the wall opposite the window but got no response. I realized that I was not only alone but isolated from the other prisoners. Before finally going to sleep on the cold cement floor, I prayed to God for a long time and asked for strength to endure what was to come. It was the uncertainty of what lay in the future that was so hard to deal with. However, I had my leaf, and I had faith that God was not going to abandon me in this place.

In the morning, as the wake-up gong was sounded, I woke to a dim light to see just how small and miserable my confinement was. From the Vietnamese voices outside the window, I realized that I was close to the "Head Shed" which contained the interrogation rooms and administrative offices. How could I endure such proximity to my tormentors?

About mid-morning, the gloom was pierced by a beam of sunlight shining through an undiscovered crack in the shutters. It struck the opposite wall with a sharp brilliance—surely a sign from God once again. Quickly I made a small paper cross from the scrap of what served as toilet paper and glued it to the wall with some rice grains just at the spot where the sun had struck. Each day, as the sunlight illuminated the little cross, I felt the presence of God and it sustained me throughout that lonely and difficult time.

Once again came the demand for a choice—cooperate or go to a worse place. All the way across the prison next to the back wall was a small shed that had been used to store coal, among other things. It was infested with ants, mosquitoes, geckos, and, at night, rats. I was finally convinced that this was really the worst place they had. Food that was barely edible to begin with was left outside the door for hours, and when I got it, it was covered with ants. I was weak from constant diarrhea, sleepless nights, and constant interrogation, humiliation, beatings, and loneliness throughout each day. After several weeks, I was very close to the end of my strength and resolve. The worst part was having no one to talk to, so my prayers were for strength and companionship. When the time came again to choose, I was not sure I could survive for long in a place worse than this shed, and I was tempted to try and get them off my back by answering a few questions. Luckily, I did not give in because their idea of the worst place was putting me in a cell with a black man. I was ordered to care for him as he was badly injured and could do nothing for himself. The Vietnamese must have thought that forcing us together in this situation would set us against each other and break us down.

Major Fred Cherry and I lived together for eight months, and the Vietnamese plan did not work. Fred nearly died several times during that time, but he was too determined and much too tough to die. He says that I saved his life, but he is the one who probably saved mine. He was indeed a gift from God and the answer to my prayers. We became lifelong friends, and it was his example of courage, patriotism, devotion to duty, and personal integrity that set a high standard during those difficult years that followed. The night we were moved apart was one of the saddest of my life, and we were both to go back into solitary confinement and endure serious torture to force our cooperation. It was strength from God and what I learned from Fred that helped me get through that terrible time.

John E. Hanson
WWII • PTO

During my experience as a POW, I developed the following creed; it has served me well in life.

1. Do the best you can with what you have.
2. If you are not in a position to help your neighbor, at least avoid harming him.
3. Value freedom. It becomes very precious once it has been lost.
4. Respect your body and mind. Feed each properly and do not abuse either.
5. Be kind to animals. This is very important. We are all creatures of God.

HE HEARD MY PRAYERS

In the summer of 1942, following the fall of Bataan and Corregidor, I was held in the main Philippine prison camp at Cabanatuan with 5,000 other captives. There were 30 to 40 men dying each day from dysentery, malaria, and starvation. The Japanese guards despised us for having surrendered instead of fighting to the death and seemed to take great delight in making life as miserable as possible for the Americans under their control.

The arithmetic of the situation indicated that all of us would be dead in a few months unless conditions improved. I did not think the Lord would answer prayers for more food or medicine, but I did pray for the strength to endure and survive. Thank God He heard my prayers!

Colonel Carlyle "Smitty" Harris
U.S. Air Force (Ret.) • Vietnam

It is difficult to express a creed or code of conduct, which guides one's life, in a few words. Everything I do, say, act, think, respond to, avoid, or consider is part of my makeup that has been formed from infancy by heredity, family, teachers, role models, reading, experiences, observations, beliefs, religious upbringing, and sometimes attitudes which I do not know if they are learned or are a basic part of one's being. The following are not necessarily in the order of importance (which may change due to the nature of the circumstance) nor are they comprehensive.

1. I believe in God and an afterlife. I believe in prayer, but I think that God rarely responds to a person in miracles we ask for. Nevertheless, He responds with gifts much more valuable than we could have ever conceived. As a POW, the torture did not stop. I wasn't reunited with my family, the pain continued, time drug on, other sick men died. But eventually nearly all the personal miracles occurred—just not on my selfish timetable. But I gained in many ways—to the extent that I now believe the POW experience was very positive in my life. I believe I have a greater enjoyment of everything in nature and in life, a stronger faith, and feel good about myself and my family relationships. I am optimistic and happy. I am better able to make good decisions. Whichever of God's character traits I may have, I believe they are stronger and less vulnerable to any temptations. I believe my prayers were answered.

2. I believe optimism and a can-do attitude are the attributes which are most important to the successful completion of almost any endeavor.

3. Integrity is one of the most important attributes one can have. Dependability and responsibility are just subsets of integrity. If one says he will do something, be somewhere at an appointed time, help with a cause, or carry out a project, failure to do so (except for impossible and unforeseen circumstances) is a direct and negative reflection of his integrity. For myself, I believe the worst thing that would destroy my self-esteem would be the knowledge that I had not told the truth or had failed to do that which I had promised to do.

4. Establishing good relationships with others (especially our family) is another almost absolute in my life. It makes me very happy to see my three children happily married, leading productive and happy lives, and instilling in their children the values which I believe are important. It is almost an affirmation that Louise and I must have done something right. Being kind to those who have no relation to me is also important.

My response to how to move from success to significance is as follows: Achieving my goals and having positive outcomes (success) is, of course, personally rewarding. Whether intended or not, what one does is observed by those with whom one comes in contact. If the achievements are considered worthy, good people will try to emulate or copy the manner in which the goals were reached. I would much rather make someone else feel important and significant.

During my incarceration in the prisons of North Vietnam, I was fortunate, even blessed, to introduce the tap code early on. *(See page 165 for a description of the tap code.)* This method of communication was very important to the entire POW group. I just happened to be the person, at the right time, with the right tool needed for communication. More importantly, I am a significant person to my wife, children (and their spouses), grandchildren, and close personal friends and that is the significance that I seek. And, of course, each of us is of great significance to God.

WELCOME HOME DAD

At two o'clock in the morning, the Air Force C-141 landed at Maxwell Air Force Base in Montgomery, Alabama. As I walked off the aircraft, my emotions were in total turmoil. I was about to meet my wife, two daughters, and a son whom I had never seen. It had been almost eight years since my F-105 fighter had been shot down over North Vietnam, and my son Lyle had been born one month later.

In Okinawa, Louise and I had purchased a very nice three-bedroom home with a fantastic view of the Pacific. About 75 feet from our large back porch was a steep bluff overlooking a small village below and Buckner Bay where a U.S. carrier and support ships often anchored. Our life was almost idyllic. Robin and Carolyn, ages four and three, laughed and played happily—often with our maid, Shiko, who was enthralled with their antics and their almost white blond hair. Louise kept busy decorating our nursery and making other preparations for the expected addition to our family. We did not know if we were going to have a little girl or a little boy, but it didn't really make any difference. Life was great.

The 67th Tactical Fighter Squadron was a very close-knit unit, including our wives. We often partied together, and the wives were a wonderful support for each other when we pilots were sent on temporary duty to Thailand, from where we flew combat missions over Laos and North Vietnam. Our Squadron commander, Lt. Colonel Robbie Risner, had been a Korean War fighter pilot, was a natural leader, and commanded respect for his living example of Christian faith. For a young fighter pilot, it couldn't get much better than flying combat missions in a sophisticated fighter with other pilots whom I knew and trusted. We were well trained, capable, and knew that we were supporting our country's mission to keep South Vietnam free from the Communists of North Vietnam.

Then, on a bombing mission, my aircraft was hit by enemy anti-aircraft fire, and I was forced to eject and parachute into hostile territory. During my incarceration, my primary responsibility was to resist any efforts by my captors to exploit me in any way for their purposes. There were times when we were tortured, denied medical attention, malnourished, kept in solitary confinement, threatened, and made to suffer both extreme heat and cold. When things were really bad, there was a hierarchy of beliefs without which we could not survive. The first was a belief in God, then our country, our fellow POWs, and our family and friends back home. We simply must not let them down—and we gained strength to prevail over a brutal enemy by our firm foundation in these beliefs. No matter what our religious practices had been prior to captivity, there were no atheists when we reached the point where we were not sure we would survive. We prayed. Almost all of us gained the strength to continue and eventually came home with our honor intact. Unfortunately, there were some who were killed or could not survive their treatment.

My thoughts and prayers were never far from my family. From later shoot-downs, including Robbie Risner, I found out that Louise had given birth to our son, Carlyle S. Harris, Jr. (Lyle for short.) As I walked down the ramp of that airplane at Maxwell Air Force Base I was thinking over all the questions that had plagued me for the last week when I found out that we were going to be released. Had Louise changed? Would Robin and Carolyn remember Dad? And the biggest unknown was Lyle. Well, I was about to find out.

I was directed to a staff car and entered the back seat—in the dark, I had not been able to see inside—and there was Louise. She had never looked more beautiful. On the way to the Officer's Quarters, she briefed me that waiting there were not only the kids but my Mom and Dad, my brother, Louise's mother, her sister and husband, Dick, and their children, and Louise's grandmother. I had hoped to spend a day or two with just Louise, perhaps in Hawaii, to catch up on all the family news so I would be better able to respond to them. But, this was exciting too. I was just bursting to see our son. As I stepped into the quarters, both Robin and Carolyn squealed and came running to jump in my arms. Oh, thank you Lord! They hadn't forgotten. They had grown to be lovely, young women—I was overcome with emotion and tears of joy rolled down my face. Then there was Lyle. I picked him up and hugged him for a long time, and it didn't bother me that he didn't hug back. I knew that would take a little time. Louise had always talked about me to the kids, and she said that when planes flew over, Lyle, even as a little boy, often remarked to his mom, "There goes Daddy." But the man picking him up was still a stranger.

I was, of course, delighted to see everyone. The whole room was almost chaos with talk and laughter. I had purchased gifts for everyone while I was at Clark Air Force Base in the Philippines, en route home. And they all had gifts for me. After about 30 or 40 minutes, while I was sitting in a large easy chair and opening a gift, I looked around for Lyle and found him in a corner just watching me. I turned and opened my arms toward him and he came running, jumped into my lap, and threw his arms around my neck in a big hug. Again, oh thank you Lord!

Gerald Harvey
WWII • ETO

As a child in Vacation Bible School, I learned this motto: "I will do the best I can with what I have, where I am, for Jesus' sake, today." This has stayed with me all my life—in the Air Force, as a prisoner of war, in school, in missionary service, in every part of my life. I also believe in setting goals ahead of where I am. As soon as I reach one, I set a new one. I have not reached all of them, but when I fall short of the goal, I look for another open door or opportunity that God always has available. I believe that God will be with you through all of life until He calls you to be with Him.

NO NEVER ALONE

It was February 16, 1945. I was the radio-gunner on the crew of a B-17 bomber. We were starting out to bomb an oil refinery at Gelsenkirchen, Germany. When we reached the target, the bombardier gave the order, "Bombs Away," but nothing happened. I could see directly into the bomb bay, and all the bombs were still there. The crew mechanic found the problem; a switch had not been thrown. When he threw the switch and the bombs fell, he was almost pulled out of the plane. While we were over the target, we were hit by flak and lost two engines. We were forced to drop out of formation and were flying alone. When we neared the coast, our pilot offered us the choice of bailing out or trying to make it back to England. We chose to stay with the plane. We began to throw out everything that could be moved in an attempt to lighten the load. When we reached the North Sea, we knew that we were not going to make it and began to prepare for a crash landing. I placed my parachute in front of my radio and put my head on it.

The pilot tried to drag the tail to slow us down, but when the nose hit the water, it was like running into a brick wall at 100 miles an hour. The plane broke in half right where I was sitting. By the time I stood up, water was up to my chest. We were only able to get one raft out of the plane. It was made to only hold four or five men, and there were nine of us. When we all climbed into the small raft, it was like a rubber innertube, and I was sitting in water up to my waist. We had sent a radio distress message and were hopeful that someone would come. We all had heard stories about the dangers of crashing in the North Sea. The water was so cold it would not take long to freeze to death. We knew that if we were in the water for more than 15 minutes, we might as well forget it. It began to get dark and no one came. We remained in the water for 12 hours.

The other men in the raft told me that several times I lost consciousness and slipped out of the raft and into the sea. They kept pulling me back onto the raft. The water was so cold that we lost all feeling from the waist down. It was like being paralyzed. All night long we sang hymns and prayed, until finally we heard a noise and saw a light. We didn't know what or who it was, but we thought it might be a ship. Then we realized that we had floated to shore. We were near the Dutch coast near the town of Haarlem. When the Germans came out and picked us up, our situation was desperate. At that point we were happy to see any living person. We were all suffering from extreme hypothermia. Our feet and our legs were so cold that none of us was able to walk.

We all realized that our prayers had been answered; survival in the North Sea for that length of time was a miracle. I thought of the song that I had sung so many times when I was growing up, "No never alone, no never alone. He promised never to leave me, never to leave me alone." We were POWs, but God had not left us alone. While we were in the water, I knew that He would be with me no matter what happened in the days ahead. That assurance stayed with me during the difficult times as a prisoner. When I came home, I knew that God had brought me through many difficult situations for a purpose. He still had something for me to do.

Betsy Herold Heimke
Internee, Philippines, Bilibid Prison

Appreciate the freedom that we enjoy as American citizens. Keep abreast of current events by executing our God-given responsibility and vote when the opportunity presents itself.

MY LITTLE AMERICAN FLAG

We had been interned by the Japanese for seven months. During that time we watched the Japanese flag flap in the warm breeze on a tall flag pole in front of the guard house. We loathed that large, red blotch that we kids called "a rotten fried egg." My mother was the chairman of the Women's Committee; therefore our small cubicle became the storehouse for lost-and-found items, outgrown clothes, curtains, and bits and pieces of cloth. As she was looking over that pile of material on the birthday of our country, she came across an unused, bright blue, square napkin. Suddenly, her patriotic zeal inspired her to make our beloved American flag. Bright red caddie shirts from the Baguio Country Club were cut into narrow strips and hand-stitched on a faded, white ironing board cover whose length determined the length of the flag. Forty-eight white stars were button-holed on the field of blue. Not having seen our American flag for several months, we had to guess which stripe was placed under the field of blue. The adored flag was clandestinely and lovingly hand-stitched by most of the women in camp, including two British ladies. Three years later on December 28, 1944, after losing 60 pounds, Mother stuffed the flag inside her bra. There it would be easily accessible in case she had to fly it to warn American pilots not to strafe our unidentifiable convey enroute on Central Luzon to Bilibid Prison in Manila.

On the memorable morning of February 4, 1945, after the Japanese left, the revered flag was publicly unfurled for all to see for the first time. We cried tears of joy and gratitude as we sang our almost forgotten *Star Spangled Banner, God Bless America,* and *God Save the King.* That night the Second Battalion of the 148th Infantry of the 37th Division stumbled onto our motley, starving group. Our initial fear was followed by euphoric joy. We did not recognize the strange helmets worn by the tall, upbeat, enthusiastic American soldiers who called themselves GIs and handed us chocolate bars, chewing gum and cigarettes. The following night, to avoid the approaching holocaust of the Battle of Manila, a rapid midnight evacuation from Bilibid ensued. Our esteemed flag was left behind and never seen again.

Mother's patriotism rubbed off on me. When we were in Camp Holmes, I hand-stitched my own precious little American flag from scraps left over from the larger one. I stashed it in my makeshift suitcase, a Baguio Country Club chaircover, and held it tightly during our rapid jeep ride away from Bilibid through the front lines of the Battle of Manila.

Many years later I was once again reminded of the cherished freedom we Americans enjoy and too often take for granted. One late night after watching a Revolutionary War movie on TV, I reflected on the three and a half years of starvation, humiliation, and deprivation that we endured in that prison camp. The movie ended with the quote by Ben Franklin, "Where liberty dwells, there is my country." We may have been physically conquered and placed in prison, but our souls never were conquered. During those long years, we prayed for liberation.

I decided to have my little flag professionally framed. On the cream colored linen mat under the flag, I cross-stitched in black silk thread Ben's words. The framed flag hangs with distinction on the paneled wall in our family room. One never truly appreciates one's flag until it has been taken away. My eternal gratitude and blessing to the gallant and brave GIs to whom we owe our lives!

Chief Warrant Officer Harland Hendrix
U.S. Air Force (Ret.) • WWII • ETO

Throughout three careers, having learned about that which breaks a man's spirit, I have always asked God's wisdom in order to lead others to faith in Him. That wisdom embodies honesty, discipline, confidence, caring, teamwork, support, motivation, a positive attitude, and a complete understanding of His blessings. Jesus came that we may have life and have it more abundantly!

IN HIM WILL I TRUST

As a young boy at home, my name was mentioned out loud by my mother and father each evening near bedtime. They were kneeling at the piano bench praying for God's help and mercies to sustain me through life. Little did I know that this season of parental concern was preparation for events beyond my control in later life. When the Gestapo caught me evading in the area of the Pyrenees Mountains, survival from inhumane treatment came only through His mercies and my knowledge that people at home (not only parents, but a loving and praying wife) were mentioning my name out loud to my Lord.

I survived many life-and-death events while thinking, "Yea, though I walk through the valley of the shadow of death, I will fear no evil. For thou art with me." Many memory verses from the Bible, which I had learned as a child, sustained me. They live in my memory today and are applied daily in decision-making, sensitivity to others, and thankfulness to my heavenly Father in the name of Jesus Christ. He is my refuge and my fortress. In Him will I trust.

Wayne Hitchcock
WWII • ETO
Past National Commander
American Ex-POWs 1997-1998

Being a Boy Scout leader for several years, I believe strongly in the Scout Oath: "On my honor I will do my best to do my duty to God and my country, and to obey the Scout Law, to help other people at all times, to keep myself physically strong, mentally awake and morally straight." What a wonderful world we would live in if everyone would subscribe to this! This puts God first and above all things.

I would also recommend the memorization or frequent reading of the poem "IF" by Rudyard Kipling. The poem ends with these well-known words: "If you can talk with crowds and keep your virtue, or walk with kings—nor lose the common touch; If neither foes nor loving friends can hurt you; If all men count with you, but none too much; If you can fill the unforgiving minute with sixty seconds' worth of distance run—Yours is the Earth and everything that's in it, and, which is more, you'll be a man, my son!"

WHAT MATTERS MOST

I grew up in Indiana and was raised on a farm. After I graduated from high school, I went to college for a short period at Ball State University in Muncie, Indiana. In 1942, I entered the service and was assigned to the Army Air Corps. After Aerial Gunnery School at Buckingham Air Base in Florida, I went overseas to Foggia, Italy, and was assigned as a tail-gunner on a B-17. On April 3, 1944, on my fourteenth mission, we were shot down over Hungary. After capture we were moved by train in boxcars to Stalag XVIIB in Krems, Austria. The camp was liberated on May 3, 1945, by Patton's 3rd Army.

As soldiers, we lived and died for the hope of peace. We lived beyond the moments of inequities and inconveniences. We lived more for the future and not the present. We lived for others rather than for ourselves. What has made this country strong and great is our willingness to sacrifice today for what tomorrow can bring in both peace and war. Always remember that when freedom is at stake, we must rise again, like we did in WWII. It matters not the wounds of battle nor the lingering pain that follows. What matters most is our commitment and devotion to our nation's freedom. Even if the cost is great, we must defend our nation when our freedom is threatened. My prayer for all time is that our country will always embody the values that made this nation great. Wounds will heal, pain will cease, but what we fought and suffered for will live forever, as long as those who come after us share the same devotion.

Colonel Roger Ingvalson
U.S. Air Force (Ret.) • Vietnam

All success is secular; all significance is spiritual. My goals in life changed after I was shot down and captured by the North Vietnamese just prior to my 40th birthday. It was on this day that Jesus Christ performed a miracle by sparing my life after ejection from my jet fighter at an extremely high speed. That day I became a Christian. My first 18 years of active duty in the US Air Force were spent attempting to achieve success in the secular world. Then, through my relationship with Christ, I realized that success was meaningless without having significance in life. Leadership by example became my motto as a military leader. My walk must equal my talk. I never gave an order without insuring that I could do it myself. After 26 years, I retired from the Air Force and formed a prison ministry. During the 15 years that I ministered to inmates, it was evident to me that unless I demonstrated a significance in my life, it was futile to expect to see a change in inmates' lives.

———

MIRACLE
It was May 28, 1968. The air war in Vietnam had been going on for three and a half years. My mission was to lead a flight to destroy a bridge in North Vietnam. We both had an air to ground missile hung under each wing. It was a good assignment—literally no defenses, or so I thought. We were successful in destroying the target. This was my 87th mission, and

with 1600 hours in the F-105, I was confident that I could hit any target. As we pulled off the target, an Air Controller requested that we hit an enemy convoy of trucks. Having a full load of 20 mm available, I jumped at the chance to destroy the trucks. My philosophy was that it was a waste of mission to engage a ground target unless I destroyed it. I believed in high speed and low altitude engagement in order to assure accuracy.

Locating the trucks, I rolled in doing approximately 500 knots, waiting until I was below 50 feet before I pulled the trigger and fired a long burst on the trucks. Then it happened—there were air defenses in the area. I heard and felt the explosion! My cockpit immediately filled with smoke. I hit the afterburner to gain valuable altitude, then pulled the canopy ejection handle to get rid of the smoke. I rocketed up to about 600 feet when my aircraft went into an uncontrollable roll. The problem was not only that I was no longer gaining altitude, but I was rapidly heading down. The situation was desperate. Ignoring ejection procedures and more by reflex, I pulled the ejection seat handle and squeezed the trigger. That's the last thing I remembered until I regained consciousness just before hitting the ground. I realized that I was doomed for capture. My freedom was about to be lost to dozens of people racing toward me, yelling in an angry foreign tongue.

As I hit the ground, my first thought and reaction was to feel for broken bones. With 15 years of fighter aircraft experience, I was fully aware of the fact that there is very little chance of survival during an emergency ejection, at high speed and low altitude, without a multitude of injuries and fractured bones. To my amazement, I had no broken bones or other injuries.

I had spent my entire 40 years of life regularly attending church, but I was not a Christian. With my knowledge of the Bible, I knew that Jesus Christ performed miracles, and there was no doubt in my mind that this was a miracle. The Lord got my attention, so in the middle of this dried-up rice paddy with dozens of angry people getting ready to capture me, I prayed that Jesus Christ would take over my life.

I was captured immediately, but because of making the most important decision of my life, I survived almost five years of torture, starvation, and loneliness as a POW. Yes, it was the worst day of my life. I lost my freedom. However, it was also the best day of my life, because I gained new hope and the promise of eternal freedom in heaven!

Lloyd Jackson
WWII • PTO

Live by the Golden Rule. Treat others the way you would like to be treated. When you meet someone who is less fortunate, always offer them a helping hand. Life is precious; don't waste it.

FREEDOM AND THE LAST BOWL OF RICE

I was born on July 18, 1915, on a farm in Missouri. When WWII began, I was in the Army serving as a medic in the Philippines. I am a survivor of the infamous Bataan Death March. The Japanese soldiers were brutal and without compassion. Those who fell out or fell behind during the march were executed; the lucky ones were shot, but others were not as fortunate. I was able to save the life of a friend by pulling his body from the dead pile. He was unable to walk so I carried him during the march. I was able to find potato peelings to feed him, which helped keep him alive. We both survived the war and maintained a life-long friendship.

I spent 1,039 days as a POW. Our daily diet, if we were lucky, consisted of one bowl of rice a day. I supplemented that by eating insects and any other varmint that I could find and catch. When I returned home, I never ate another bowl of rice.

One source of encouragement during my captivity was to be allowed to fill out a Red Cross postcard that would be mailed to my family, giving them some news about our condition. The card had a small box that could be checked that indicated if we were well or if we were sick. The postcard gave me hope and made me feel like I had a connection with the outside world and with my family.

I believe my survival as a prisoner of war was related to my faith. We were able to have church on Sunday. It was one thing that we could depend on. Life without a periodic source of hope makes it difficult to survive. Someone was always willing to lead the worship service. If one of the leaders died, another prisoner would take their place and lead the service. Worship and the willingness of others to help and to care for each other was a great source of hope.

When I joined the service, I was six feet tall and weighed 200 pounds. When we were rescued, I weighed only 78 pounds and was 5' 10" tall. We often take life for granted. Always remember that life, good health, friends, and a loving family are each a special blessing.

Colonel Harold Johnson
U.S. Air Force (Ret.) • Vietnam

My advice for life is always do what is right, commit yourself to a life of complete honesty and stand up for what you believe in, no matter the circumstance. Have faith in God and trust in Him, putting God first, then country, and both above self.

BLESSED IS THE MAN

I grew up on a small farm in Iowa. My grandfather never learned to read or write, and my father only had a sixth grade education, but they were able to develop in me the spirit gained from hard work, a sense of values, a dedication to purpose, and a feeling of patriotism.

My family weren't church-going people, so I didn't have a development or appreciation of a religious faith until and during the six years of my captivity in North Vietnam. It was there that I grew to understand why all men must find something greater than themselves to look up to and worship. My acceptance there of Jesus Christ as my Savior began a personal journey of enlightenment and guidance. The spiritual uplift gave me valuable insight and armed me with understanding. The excellent guidance I gained is best demonstrated by one of my favorite Bible verses: "Blessed is the man that walketh not in the counsel of the ungodly, nor standeth in the way of sinners, nor sitteth in the seat of the scornful. But his delight is in the law of the Lord; and in His law doth he meditate day and night" (Psalm 1:1-2).

Life's lessons have taught me that leadership is of the spirit; management is of the mind. All people can be educated and trained to use the systems and methods available to organize and manage things. Only the strongly developed spirit in an individual can make a individual an effective leader of people. I have experienced it in myself and witnessed this spirit in the leadership of others which leads me to the conclusion that there are no great men—only great challenges to be met. Personal characteristics such as integrity, self-discipline, and emotional stability provide a person with the courage necessary to deal with all the challenges they encounter. God's grace massages the spirit of each individual in such a way that it highlights those characteristics of leadership necessary at any moment of trial and allows us to cope.

Colonel Sam Johnson
U.S. Air Force (Ret.) • Vietnam

I spent 29 years in the Air Force and was proud to answer my nation's call to service in Korea and in Vietnam. The Air Force taught me the value of duty, honor, and country. And by its nature, the military is committed to excellence and success. We send young men to battle to fight for our freedom and for democracy to win. We should all strive for success, but what is it that makes us significant?

During my captivity I realized that my significance comes from God. I am nothing without Him, and while my military training prepared me well for my years of captivity, it was God who allowed my survival.

HIS MERCIES ARE NEW EVERY MORNING

As a Prisoner of War for nearly seven years, I went through some difficult times. I spent 42 months in solitary confinement and 74 days in stocks. I told about my days as a POW in my book, *Captive Warrior: A Vietnam POW's Story.*

On the evening of my 74th day in stocks, I stared at the boarded-up window of my cell. It had been so long since I had seen the sky and the sun. My eyes blurred with tears, and at that moment, I felt suddenly finished. It was over; I couldn't fight any more. I remember thinking as I fell asleep, exhausted and defeated, that it would be okay if I never woke up again.

Late that night a typhoon tore through the city of Hanoi, ripping roofs off buildings and lashing the prison courtyard with wind and slicing rain. I awoke to the sounds of breaking glass and slamming window shutters. The floor of my cell was filled with water, and I huddled against the wall, as far away from the incoming rain as the leg stocks would allow me. The violence of the storm stirred something inside me, and I began to pray like I had never prayed before. Long after the storm subsided, I lay on my bunk, drenched from the rain, and strangely at peace in the darkness.

I awoke the next morning to see my cell flooded with the first bright streaks of dawn. The storm had ripped the boards off my window, and for the first time in more than two months, sparkling rays of light danced a celebration in my tiny room. I had an overwhelming sense of the presence of God in that moment. He was with me, and He would be faithful. His fresh supply of mercy was pouring into my cell with all the reality of the sun's shining rays. I understood the Bible verse I learned as a child: "His mercies are new every morning." I was convinced that He would be sufficient for me; He would see me through.

Major Kenneth Jones
U.S. Air Force (Ret.) • WWII • ETO

If I was to offer my creed or code of conduct for life, I would offer the advice given to me by my grandparents. I was raised by my grandparents, the most lovable couple who lived by the motto, "Be honest, truthful, and do unto others as you would have them do unto you, and God will take care of you and yours." I have tried to live up to their motto and believe that I have, for God has most certainly taken care of me and mine.

While my children were growing up, I would tell them to never give up and that your mind is your greatest asset and also your greatest weapon. You can overcome just about anything, if you put your mind to it.

I would also offer this as practical advice: Do the best you can. If that doesn't work, then look at the situation from a different angle; the answer will come to you. Don't let someone tell you that you can't do something. The only thing that will stop you from achieving your goals is you.

NEVER, NEVER EVER, GIVE UP

On August 12, 1943, I was on my 17th combat mission as a ball-turret gunner when my B-17 and another plane from our squadron collided at 30,000 feet. Before the collision, our plane was attacked by ME-109s from the Hermann Goering Fighter Squadron. Along with four of my crew members, I was wounded during the attack. After our plane crashed, we were taken to a German military hospital. I remained in the hospital for about six weeks for treatment of injuries, which included a broken back. I was then transferred to Stalag VI.

I was able to escape, and I eventually made my way to the Rhine river. I was still on crutches and in significant pain. I hobbled for miles, all the time trying to avoid capture. I believed it was my duty to try to escape. When I reached the river, I walked up and down the bank trying to find a place shallow enough to cross. To complicate the situation, I had never learned how to swim. I might have made it if I had found a shallow spot in the river. But it was not to be. I was recaptured and sent to Buchenwald to Dulag Luft. I spent five days in a boxcar that traveled to Stalag XVIIB in Kerms. In April 1945, Stalag XVIIB was evacuated, and we were forced marched from Kerms to Brauna, Austria. It was in Austria that I was liberated by the 13th Army Division of the U.S. 3rd Army on the May 2, 1945.

After the war I remained in the Air Force and was blessed to be able to serve the nation in uniform for 33 years. I served in both Korea and Vietnam. Throughout my life, God has always taken care of me and my family!

Colonel George Juskalian
U.S. Army (Ret.) • WWII • ETO

At the end of WWII, I was privileged to be present when Chief of Staff of the Army, George C. Marshall, assembled his staff in his office in the Pentagon to thank them for their service and to bid them farewell. One phrase that he used in thanking them was their integrity of effort. As I later reflected on those words, I realized that they were, in fact, a succinct statement of his own distinguished service to the nation. His staff had observed that quality in him and had responded in kind. From that time on, I adopted those words as my personal code of conduct because they embodied the values—honesty, loyalty, respect for others, courage, discipline, hard work—that I hold dear and which, in the eyes of my fellowman, I trust I have fulfilled.

THE PRAYERS OF A MOTHER

As our POW column was skirting the southern border of Nuremberg on our way to Moosberg in the waning days of the war, American bombers suddenly appeared overhead and began plastering a railroad marshalling yard about a mile ahead. We cheered them on with our harmless anger directed toward the dispirited guards. Just as the final V-shaped sorties of the formation approached our position, the lead plane dropped its flare, which was the signal for all planes to drop their bombs. They were directly above us! We hit the dirt as the bombs rained toward us, sounding like the volley of a hundred cannons. My thoughts turned immediately to my mother. My poor mother, I thought. She had been waiting on edge these past two years for my return. Now with the war about to end, was I about to die? If it came to that, I knew there would be not one death but two, for her soul and her will to live would die with me. Thank God I was spared. For this I credit my mother. She was a simple woman, a God-loving, God-fearing woman from whom the grace of God must have surged incomprehensibly to save me.

J. Lawrence King
WWII • ETO

My advice for life is: Always do what you know is right and always be honest. Make a commitment to God and stand by that commitment. Have faith in and trust in God. In a trench in France during WWII, I renewed my trust and faith in God and promised to serve Him if I lived through the war—not a bargain, but a promise. I serve Him in whatever way I can, for He is my leader and source of my life. God loves you, too.

I WILL FEAR NO EVIL

I was fortunate to grow up in a Christian home where my mother and father lived by their word and example and believed in Proverbs 22:6, "Train up a child in the way he should go: and when he is old, he will not depart from it." This proved to be true with all five children. The three sons were all in combat in Europe at the same time, and each of us returned.

I was in the Army Enlisted Reserve in college prior to being called to active duty on November 21, 1943, four months after becoming eligible for military service at 18 years old. After an abbreviated basic training, I was assigned to the Army Specialized Training Program to prepare for combat. I was part of an anti-tank company, in the 94th Division. In France we were part of the Third Army under the command of General Patton. As the Battle of the Bulge was contained, we started retaking territory along the infamous WWI Siegfried Line. In January 1945, we were experiencing one of the coldest winters on record. The snow depth was 15-18 inches as we approached the town of Orsholz in the Saar Valley. The mission went from bad to worse and 300 of us were captured.

Initially I spent time in a hospital at Saint Wendel, Germany, and was then moved to a Stalag in Nuremberg and then moved again to a Stalag at Hammerburg, where I was assigned to a small work detail. One morning as we were going out to work, another group of POWs was returning. As we passed they yelled, "Don't work! It's defense emplacements—we don't have to do that!" Arriving where the earlier detail had been, we could see the outline of a rectangular, foxhole-shaped clearing that had been made.

The German guard handed me a shovel, pointing his rifle at the ground and shouted, "Dig!" I responded by saying, "Nein." As we sat stubbornly on the snow-covered ground refusing to dig, he again commanded, "Dig!" When I didn't move, he raised his rifle and placed the muzzle to the side of my head. The sound of the bolt forcing a round into the chamber was loud and unmistakable. Again I replied, "Nein." The word came out of my mouth only by the strength of God. I never felt like I was a brave person, but I felt God's presence, giving me strength.

I don't know why he didn't shoot, but he began to lower the rifle from the side of my head. He immediately raised it again and brought the weapon down across my shoulder, knocking me flat on the frozen ground. I don't remember the pain as much as I remember the satisfaction that I experienced feeling that this was one small battle I had won for my country, and it was done with God's help. Shortly, our Camp Commander arrived with some German officers and said, "I know what you think, and you may even be right, but we cannot prove that these foxholes are meant to be used as air raid shelters, so you will have to dig, but take my advice, dig real slow.'

As I reflect on my experience as a POW, I don't know why I came back and others didn't, but I am glad that I knew Jesus well enough to rely on Him at a time when there seemed to be no hope. He was there for us. God through Jesus paid the price for our sins. So often we forget to thank Him for His gifts and we also fail to ask Him for His help. In Psalm 23:4 it says, "Yea though I walk through the valley of the shadow of death, I will fear no evil: for thou art with me." I was a scared, 19 year old boy far from home who became a man overnight. He was with me then, and 60 years later He is still with me.

John Klumpp
WWII • ETO

My creed or code of conduct is the same advice that I still remember my mother telling me. It is: Anything worth doing, is worth doing right. The advice is from the Scripture, Ecclesiastes 9:10, "Whatsoever thy hand findeth to do, do it with thy might."

GIVE GOD THE GLORY

Like many combat veterans, I really don't understand why some came back and others did not. Six out of nine of my crew died from flak wounds and/or from crashing into a pine forest. I was one of only three who survived and have given God credit and the glory for saving and guiding me for a purpose. Still, after all these years, I do not know what that purpose is, but I believe that a power greater than anything I have ever felt has given me guidance since then. I continue to strive to do what is right and honorable in hope that some day I may accomplish what the Lord has in mind for me.

Frank Kravetz
WWII • ETO

Our youth need to know that freedom is not free! My captors could not deny me my prayers to God. I fashioned a set of Rosary Beads, with which I prayed, from a piece of string. My strong faith, along with love of country and love of family, was my source of strength for my survival.

CHRISTMAS MASS

I grew up in East Pittsburgh, Pennsylvania. I entered the Army Air Corps in November 1943. I was assigned to the 457th Bomb Group of the 8th Air Force, stationed in England. On November 2, 1944, we took off from Glatton Air Force Base as part of an air strike against German oil refineries. Immediately after we dropped our bombs we were attacked by enemy fighters. I was wounded in both legs from shrapnel. Our B-17 was damaged so badly that we were flying with only one engine. Fortunately the pilot was able to keep the plane airborne long enough to allow us to bail out over Hannover, Germany.

I was immediately captured and sent to a hospital that was set up in an old school. By Christmas Day the hospital was jammed with new patients, mostly young American soldiers wounded in the German offensive known as the Battle of the Bulge. During this period of time, I was convinced that that they were going to have to amputate one of my legs because it had turned black. I was fortunate because a German surgeon saved my leg. I still remember that Christmas because the Germans allowed us a special midnight Mass in my hospital ward. I am sure that my faith was the source of strength allowing me to survive.

I was transferred to Stalag XIIID. After several weeks I had to make a 15-day forced march to Stalag VIIA in Moosberg, Germany. By the time we were liberated, my weight had dropped from 175 pounds to 125 pounds.

Technical Sergeant Clarence Larson
U.S. Air Force (Ret.) • WWII • PTO

Having been a POW for nearly four years, many thoughts of the reasons for my survival come back to me from time to time. One thought was that I never gave up. My father often made a remark that I often think of to this day—"It could be worse!" There were times during my captivity when I almost gave up, but thankfully never did.

One night a group of men (including me) fell asleep. When I awoke because of artillery fire, I discovered that the men on my left and on my right were both dead. The thought came to me that someone was watching over me, and that someone was God. During many close calls with death, I always looked upwards and said, "Thank you, God!"

I have given numerous speeches in high schools and different organizations about my survival. When I am asked how I survived, I don't say anything. I simply point to the sky, and they understand that it was God who watched over me. My final words are about our flag which I pull out of my pocket and wave back and forth saying, "Honor your flag. It spells freedom—yours and mine—and it comes at a terrible price.

THANK YOU, GOD

My mother and father had a great influence on my life. They always made sure that we went to church on Sunday. They also helped me with my lessons prior to my confirmation. I was born in Randall, Iowa, but the family moved to Minnesota when I was two years old. We were a farming family, and I was a farmer before I joined the military. I joined the Army in November 1939. I left the farm early in the morning and headed to St Paul. From St. Paul I was sent to California and remained there for several weeks prior to my being shipped to the Philippine Islands. The trip from California took 24 days. I still remember being seasick much of the time.

We arrived in Manila, in February 1940. I was doing well and glad to be in the Army. During this assignment, we began to hear rumors about the possibility of war, and then on December 7, 1941, the Japanese bombed Pearl Harbor. From there they attacked the Philippines, bombing the air base at Nichols Field where I was stationed. I would have shipped back to the United States in only a few months, but because of the war I ended up being captured by the Japanese on April 9, 1942. I will never forget that day when I lost my freedom and wondered what my future would hold.

I was on the "Death March" that began at Bataan. It was brutal. I experienced many instances where I came close to being killed by the Japanese. During the march, I thought about my days growing up on the farm, and I remembered when mom and dad made sure that we were in church and Sunday school. It was during this time that I believe God really became Lord of my life. I realized that I had escaped death along that march many times. God was with me and comforted me.

I remember many close calls during that period of time. We were frequently shelled during the night. One night I took my army blanket to a place that I felt would be safe from artillery fire. I placed a stick in each corner of the blanket so it would not move. Hoping to get some sleep, I laid down on the blanket. As the shelling began again, I jumped up, running for cover. When the shelling stopped and I returned to retrieve my blanket, it was in shreds. Like so many times before, I looked heavenward and said, "Thank you, God."

During my captivity, I often reflected on my mom and dad and how they raised me, and I found comfort knowing that they were always praying for me. I remember so well the day that I returned home. I was convinced and I knew with all my heart that God was with me and that His plan was for me to come home to my family. I know now, and I knew then, that I was saved from death many times. I still look heavenward and say, "Thank you, God."

Richard Lockhart
WWII • ETO

My motto for life is: Always work hard, it makes life interesting, and it will give you a reason to get up each morning.

WE GAVE OUR TODAY

When World War II began, I was eager to be in it, and in fact, enlisted and volunteered for the infantry. In due course, I found myself a casualty during the Battle of the Bulge and became a POW. I will not attempt to describe these combat conditions in December 1944, the "Ardennes Snow March," or the four days and nights we were jammed into boxcars with no food or water (and being bombed by our own Air Force in the process). Suffice it to say, along with several thousand other GIs, I found myself entering the gates of Stalag IXB, Bad Orb, Germany, on December 26.

Stalag IXB was a very primitive camp, housing several thousand Russian, Serbian and French soldiers. It was reserved for Privates and Private First Class soldiers only. In the American compound, there were no American officers, except a Protestant and a Catholic Chaplain and a dentist. There were no medical facilities, no sanitary services, no heat, and not much grass soup. Men died every day.

Most Americans believe the Holocaust happened only to European civilians. That is not the case. In Stalag IXB, U.S. soldiers who were Jewish were, despite our protests, separated from the rest of us. Soon thereafter, they were taken out of the camp, destination unknown. After the war, I learned they were shipped to slave labor camps—not to a POW camp—and few survived.

You might wonder how the Germans identified the Jewish GIs. The answer is that the GIs volunteered such facts. Frankly, it is something I have never understood to this day. Was it done as a affirmation of their culture and religion? Was it done out of naiveté? Was it done out of a false sense that because they were American soldiers, that would protect them? After all these years, I still do not know. What I do know is that it happened. It demonstrates once again the enormous capacity of some to impose the cruelest of punishments on others, solely because of differences in race, religion, nationality, or culture.

There is an inscription on a monument in a WWII cemetery that reads, "When you go home, tell them of us and say, 'For your tomorrow, we gave our today.'"

Benedict Lohman
WWII • PTO

I believe my survival as a Japanese prisoner of war is directly related to my faith. I knew I had family praying for me. My advice for life would be: Have faith in God.

OUR PRAYERS WERE
HEARD AND ANSWERED

I enlisted in the U.S. Marine Corps on January 5, 1940, and I went to boot camp in San Diego. My first duty station was Shanghai, China, at the international settlement in the American Sector E. The Regiment evacuated that station in November 1941 and moved to Olongapoo, in the Philippine Islands. When the Japanese attacked the Philippines and landed at Lingalon Gulf, we shoved off for the Lingalon Gulf at Marvalis, the tip of the Bataan Peninsula. General McArthur took command of the 4th Regiment and ordered the Marines to set up beach defenses on the island of Corregidor.

As the Japanese moved toward Manila, the Philippine and American troops retreated to the Bataan Peninsula. The battle for Bataan lasted until April 9th, and on May 6th the Philippines and the island of Corregidor surrendered. With the surrender, Japan controlled the entire South Pacific. I was sent to Japan on the Corral Maru. Initially I worked in the shipyards of Osaka, Japan. But when the bombings began, I was moved to the copper mines in the mountains of Japan.

Death, starvation, sickness, lack of medicine, and cruel guards were a part of our daily existence. The situation was so bad that we were left with almost no hope. When you have no hope, you don't survive. But I did survive. I prayed to Saint Jude, the patron saint of the hopeless, every night. As a Catholic, I said "Hail Marys" and "Our Fathers" and sought protection from my Guardian Angel. The word in my home town of Lansing, Kansas was that "I was a goner." My mother must have been on her knees the entire time. When I walked into the door of my home for the first time in six years, my mother knew that our prayers had been heard and answered.

Cordino Longiotti
WWII • ETO

I am proud to be a veteran and to have fought for the freedom of the USA. I was willing to fight for freedom, and to give my life if necessary, but by the grace of God, I am here today. We truly are one nation under God, with liberty and justice for all! We may have our faults, but we are still the greatest country in the world. Regardless of any faults this nation may have, it is the only place in the world where I would want to live, and it is still worth fighting for. I would encourage everyone to read about the history of our great nation. Wars were fought for our freedom, and brave men and women gave their lives so we can have that freedom. Dying for freedom is not the worst thing that could happen, dying for freedom and being forgotten is.

GOD WAS WITH US

After a short rest in the rear, we once again moved to the front on the night of February 16, 1944. We dug in along the Albana-Anzio road that leads to the city of Anzio. We were told to hold the line at all cost. As night turned to day, the German Luftwaffe bombed and strafed our position the entire day. On the night of the 17th, the Germans used flares to light the sky as they continued their bombardment with artillery, rockets, and mortars. The enemy was trying to destroy our position prior to a morning attack.

When morning finally came, we were surprised to learn that during the night the rifle company that we were supposed to support had pulled back, and we were far forward and alone. It was only later that we found out that the 1st Battalion of the 179th Infantry was practically destroyed during the night, and that forced the rifle company to pull back. We also learned that many of the soldiers in the rifle company had been killed or captured. Although our job was to support the rifle company, we had been abandoned and left behind in the confusion of the artillery bombardment.

Our far forward position was complicated by daylight, making us feel like sitting ducks, in no man's land between the enemy to our front and our own troops in the rear. We had no way to communicate, so our two machine gun squads sat completely alone. By this time the artillery, mortar, and machine gun fire seemed to be coming at us from every direction. There was fire from our troops in the rear and from the Germans to our front.

Approximately 200 yards to our right there was a German tank firing 88mm shells point blank at our position. Our machine gun was knocked out; the only weapons we had left to defend ourselves was a carbine and my .45-caliber pistol. Our situation was desperate. As time passed we hoped for a break in the fire so we could make a run for it, but that break never came.

Shortly after daybreak the morning of February 18, five German soldiers who had circled around behind us suddenly charged the position with fixed bayonets, yelling *"Raus, Haende in die Luft!"* As soon as I stood, a German soldier jumped in the foxhole and grabbed my .45-caliber automatic pistol. Almost without exception when the Germans approached a machine gun emplacement, they would try to destroy the emplacement with grenades. For whatever reason they did not do so this time and we were spared. In only moments there were charging German soldiers everywhere. It appeared to be an entire division. It was then that I realized that if those five German soldiers had not come from behind us, we would have never made if out alive. Right then and there I gave God the credit for keeping us alive. God was with us.

David Ludlum
Korea

I was released from captivity on April 20, 1952. In 1957 I went to South Korea to begin the first of two lay missionary terms helping orphans of the Korean War. For 18 years I supplied Christian books and Bibles to Third World pastors and schools. In 1985, I married a Filipino lady and eventually moved to the Philippines to work with churches there. My advice for life is: Love God and love people. Always treat others the way you want to be treated. God does have a plan for your life...be willing to submit yourself to His plan.

OH GOD, YOU'VE GOT TO HELP ME!

During the Korean War, I was in the Army, assigned to the 2nd Infantry Division, 38th Regiment, C Company of the 1st Battalion. I was captured by the Chinese Communists and became a prisoner of war on May 18, 1951. Twelve days later I was able to escape with a friend but we were recaptured after five days of freedom. Sometime around the 1st of July we arrived at "Mining Camp," (some called it "Bean Camp"). Two weeks later the larger group with whom I had first been captured arrived. It was not long before men in the group began to die from disease and lack of food. This continued throughout the summer.

One day I began to notice that my throat was swelling due to a tooth abscess. As the abscess increased in size, I was unable to eat or drink; even breathing was difficult. I was growing weaker by the day and on the 12th day I decided that I had to get up. I had a strong will to live but knew that if I couldn't get food and water down, I would die. That afternoon I stood and used all of my remaining strength to go outside—I walked about 50 feet. The short distance took all my strength and 30 minutes to complete. Outside I sat down on a rock and lowered my head in despair. A thought came into my head. I looked up into the sky and said, "Oh God, you've got to help me!" My eyes began to fill with tears as I lowered my head again. All of a sudden, a bitter-tasting liquid filled my mouth and I realized the large abscess had begun to drain. My prayer had been answered. I was once again able to take limited amounts of food and water, starting my road to recovery.

I was moved to Camp One Hospital, formerly a Buddhist temple. A Chinese doctor visited the room I was in and inquired about the small black books beside the bedmat of many of the patients. The book was the New Testament, given to us by front-line chaplains. I picked up my New Testament, stood up, and walked over to him and let him look at the small Bible. He looked at it briefly and returned it to me. Over the weeks that he came to visit, I began to talk to him. (I was being treated for beriberi and tuberculosis.) After his rounds, I often followed him outside to visit. He began to look up verses and passages in my New Testament. Up to then, I had not really read much of the Bible. After he left, I looked up the verses that he told me to find. Over time my faith began to increase and in December 1952, while at the POW hospital, I committed my life fully to God. I said, "Oh God, if you will let me return home, I promise that I will serve you for the rest of my life." By Christmas, I was too ill to eat the POWs food. About midnight the doctor came to my bedside and hand-fed me sweet cake and milk from his own rations. When I had gained enough strength to leave the hospital, he walked with me as we left the hospital compound. As we walked toward the camp headquarters, he told me to open my New Testament to Romans 13. He told me that he had seen a change in my life as he explained how to live a Christian life. Reaching the camp headquarters, I climbed into a truck. It seems strange to have become a soldier, to have fought in a war, to have become a POW and to meet a Chinese physician who not only helped save my life but also helped to direct me along the path to becoming a Christian.

Leonard Lutjen
WWII • ETO

My advice for life is: Always be honest. I grew up during a time when the expression, "Your word is your bond," was accepted as a traditional American value. In life we will all have the opportunity to be a leader and a follower. As a leader you should never ask someone to do something that you are unwilling to do. My spiritual advice is: Have faith in God and always trust in Him!

HE WAS WITH ME

I entered the Army on August 12, 1943, and was assigned to the 90th Infantry Division and the 3rd Army. I can remember many times when I found myself in harm's way yet, by the grace of God, I was spared. My experience as a prisoner of war is different than most. I was wounded so severely that I was a patient in a POW hospital in Renne, France.

During the attack on Beau Coudray, I was shot in the head by a sniper. I was behind my machine gun when I was hit in the mouth. My mouth must have been open at the time because the bullet went between my teeth, missed my tongue, and exited below my right ear. The bullet fractured my jaw and tore my uniform off my right shoulder. I am convinced that my life was spared because I had a guardian angel with me!

Frank Mace
WWII • PTO

Live by the Golden Rule; an act of kindness will teach more about the love of God than many sermons. Trust completely in God, you never have to be afraid when you are in His hands. Always remember that when you are afraid, Jesus will hear even the faintest cry. All you have to do is be willing to surrender your fears to the Lord. To find God, you have to first seek Him.

WAKE ISLAND

I grew up on a farm. Some of my favorite memories center around the nights when our family would gather in a circle around my mother as she played the organ and the family would sing. Every Sunday we traveled five miles to Sunday school and church. We had a wagon that was pulled by a team of horses. We had 25 head of cattle, and I sang to them when I herded them back to the farm. I still remember one stormy day when I rode my horse, Blacky, to get the cattle. During the storm, lightning struck the fence and jumped from the fence, striking Blacky in the neck just after I had jumped off.

I started my ROTC training when I was 17; after two years I had the ROTC rating of a 1st Lieutenant. During my summers off I worked in construction. The contractor that I was working for bid on a job in the South Pacific. The bid was accepted, and he offered me a job as carpenter foreman if I would go. The money he offered was significantly more than I could make as an ROTC cadet, so I took the job and headed to the South Pacific and Wake Island 48 hours after I was offered the job.

On January 9, 1940, I arrived on Wake Island. In August about 350 Marines landed on the island and another 100 landed in late October. Eleven months after I arrived there the Japanese bombed Pearl Harbor, and we found ourselves at war with Japan. The Major in charge of the Marines swore all the civilian construction workers into the Marine Corps. Later a Navy Commander came and told us that he was in charge and swore us into the Navy. The Japanese began their attack on Wake on December 8, 1941, and by December 23 we were out of ammunition.

When the Japanese took us as prisoners, they killed many of the civilians and Marines that they had captured. Those of us who survived were put on ships and taken to Japan. I was a POW for 44 months.

John Maher
WWII • ETO

My advice for life is: always be honest! I believe honesty is one of the most important traits an individual can have. By being honest, everyone you meet and everyone you know will realize that when you say something, you are speaking the truth. Commit yourself to God and to country.

THE MAN UPSTAIRS

I was born and reared in the small town of Watermeet, Michigan. It was a small and close-knit community where everyone knew each other. Growing up, there seemed to be a common love and positive feelings for everyone in the community. No one that I knew had an abundance of material possessions. I was almost 6 foot tall before I went to high school and was able to get a few jobs earlier than most due to my size. This allowed me to buy most of my clothes and athletic equipment before I even started high school. After I completed high school, I entered St. Norbert College in West DePere, Wisconsin. While I was in college, Pearl Harbor was attacked. I felt overwhelmed with a feeling of duty to country and on September 9, 1942, I enlisted in the Army.

Ultimately I was assigned to I Company, 143rd Infantry of the 36th Infantry Division. Only a few in my unit survived the initial invasion of

Europe at Salerno, Italy, and that campaign. Part of the problem was we were foot soldiers fighting against a mechanized infantry. For those of us who survived, we continued on to Altavilla. Our unit continued to be depleted, and we found ourselves with fewer and fewer soldiers who could still fight. The situation was critical. It seemed like we were out of men, out of ammo, and in a battle fighting for our lives when I was captured.

After I was captured I was eventually interrogated by a German officer. As I approached the officer, I thought he looked familiar. In fairly good English he informed me that I would no longer have to worry, and he said, "For you the war is over; you will be interrogated and then go to an area like the 'Book Cadillac' hotel in Detroit, and wait to be shipped home after the war is over." All of a sudden it dawned on me! The German officer had been a supervisor at the Monroe Nursery in Monroe, Michigan, and had done landscaping at my uncle's new home in Saline, Michigan. There were a lot of people of German descent in that area and apparently he was one who had answered the call by Hitler to return to the fatherland.

I was a guest of Adolf for 19 months. I tried to live by the soldier's Code of Conduct. During the forced marches, I carried the packs and gear of other men who were wounded, weak, and exhausted. I believe this enabled some of the men to survive. We can always do something to help others who are in need.

When you have "The Man Upstairs" walking with you, the road of life is much easier. Growing up in the Upper Peninsula of Michigan, I had some knowledge of what it would take to survive in the freezing temperatures, snow and the long winter. I believe these skills and that knowledge helped us survive that winter. When I was liberated I weighed only 132 pounds, down from my normal 196 pounds. When I returned home I found out that the Honor Roll at Watermeet High School and St. Norbert College had me listed as killed in action. It took some doing, but I was finally able to get the "MIA" changed to "Returned."

James McCahon
WWII • PTO

Live by the Golden Rule. Treat others the way you would want to be treated. We are commanded to love God and to love our neighbor.

FAITH, HOPE AND CHARITY

My experiences as a survivor of the Bataan Campaign, three and one half years of Japanese prison camps, and the sinking of two "Hellships," the Oryoku Maru and the Enoura Maru, proved to me that these three essentials, faith, hope and charity, are indispensable to survival.

One of my first memories as a child was being taught that God is everywhere and is aware of our every thought and deed. I believe that this ubiquitous God has taught us, by the written Word, the difference between right and wrong. This has been my guide through life. One must have an unyielding faith in God and have the courage to do what is right no matter what the temptations might be to do otherwise.

One must never lose hope that the strength of God is a part of each individual and prayer will release that strength. To give up hope in life's efforts means failure. To give up hope as a Japanese prisoner of war meant death.

There is a demand on each individual to share his fortune with others. No matter how difficult one's life may become, there is always someone less fortunate. Share and be prayerfully thankful for those who share with you when you are in need.

This same philosophy is a guide for all of life's situations. It is essential for success in one's profession as well as any other aspect of life.

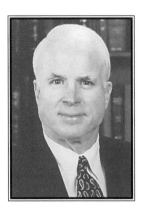

John McCain
Vietnam

Soon after I became an involuntary guest of the Democratic Republic of Vietnam, my host tried to persuade me to make a tape recording in which I would denounce my country's cause. When I resisted, they entreated me to do so by promising me that no one would know of my disloyalty. I responded, "But I would know." Virtually all my comrades who shared my situation responded the same way.

There may be times in your life when the consequences of your devotion to duty are so dire that you will be tempted to abandon it. There may be times when truly only you will know. But you will resist. I know you will. I know this because I have seen how profoundly human strength is empowered by the standards of our traditions.

I have watched men suffer the anguish of imprisonment, defy appalling human cruelty until further resistance is impossible, break for a moment, and then recover inhuman strength to defy their enemies once more. All these things and more I have seen. I will go to my grave in gratitude to my Creator for allowing me to stand witness to such courage and honor.

THE PLEDGE OF ALLEGIANCE

As you may know, I spent five and one half years as a prisoner of war during the Vietnam war. This experience is described in my book, *Faith of My Fathers*. In the early years of our imprisonment, the North Vietnamese kept us in solitary confinement or with two or three to a cell. In 1971, the North Vietnamese moved us from these conditions of isolation into large rooms with as many as 30 to 40 men to a room. This was, as you can imagine, a wonderful change and was a direct result of the efforts of millions of Americans on behalf of a few hundred POWs 10,000 miles from home.

One of the men who moved into my room was a young man named Mike Christian. Mike came from a small town near Selma, Alabama. He hadn't worn a pair of shoes until he was 13 years old. At 17, he enlisted in the U.S. Navy. He later earned a commission by going to Officer Candidate School. He then became a Naval Flight Officer and was shot down and captured in 1967. Mike had a keen and deep appreciation of the opportunities this country and our military provide for people who want to work and want to succeed.

As part of the change in treatment, the Vietnamese allowed some prisoners to receive packages from home. In some of these packages were handkerchiefs, scarves, and other items of clothing. Mike got himself a bamboo needle. Over a period of a couple of months, he created an American flag and sewed it on the inside of his shirt. Every afternoon, before we had a bowl of soup, we would hang Mike's shirt on the wall of the cell and say the Pledge of Allegiance. I know the Pledge of Allegiance may not seem the most important part of our day now, but I can assure you that in that stark cell it was indeed the most important and meaningful event.

One day the Vietnamese searched our cell, as they did periodically, and discovered Mike's shirt with the flag sewn inside and removed it. That evening they returned, opened the door of the cell, and for the benefit of all of us, beat Mike Christian severely for the next couple of hours. Then they opened the door of the cell once again and threw him back in. We cleaned him up as best as we could.

The cell in which we lived had a concrete slab in the middle on which we slept. Four naked light bulbs hung in each corner of the room. As I said, we tried to clean up Mike as well as we could. After the excitement died down, I looked in the corner of the room, and sitting there beneath that dim light bulb with a piece of red cloth, another shirt and his bamboo needle, was my friend, Mike Christian. He was sitting there with his eyes almost swollen shut from the beating he had received, making another American flag. He was not making the flag because it made Mike Christian feel better. He was making that flag because he knew how important it was to us to be able to pledge our allegiance to our flag and country.

So, the next time you say the Pledge of Allegiance, you must never forget the sacrifice and courage that thousands of Americans have made to build our nation and promote freedom around the world. You must remember our duty, our honor, our country!

PRISONER OF WAR MEDAL

Obverse: In the center of a bronze medallion one and 3/8 inches in diameter, an eagle is shown with its wings displayed. Forming a circle around the eagle and following the contour of the medal, barbed wire and bayonet points may be seen. The eagle is the American bald eagle and represents the United States in general and the individual prisoners of war in particular. It is standing with pride and dignity, continually on the alert for the opportunity to seize hold of beloved freedom.

Reverse: The reverse has the inscription AWARDED TO around the top and FOR HONORABLE SERVICE WHILE A PRISONER OF WAR across the center in three lines with a space between the two inscriptions for engraving the name of the recipient. The shield of the Coat of Arms of the United States is centered on the lower part of the reverse side with the inscription UNITED STATES OF AMERICA around the bottom of the medal.

Ribbon: The ribbon to the Prisoner of War Medal is 1-3/8 inches wide and consists of a central band of black edged in white. The edge stripes of the ribbon are composed of pinstripes of red, white, and blue (with the red forming the outer edge of the ribbon). The red, white, and blue edge stripes represent the United States; the larger white stripes represent hope, and the black center stripe alludes to the bleakness of confinement as a prisoner of war.

Captain Eugene "Red" McDaniel
U.S. Navy (Ret.) • Vietnam

Success becomes significance when it fits into God's plan, when our accomplishments somehow further His kingdom here on earth. Often that kind of significant success is not seen as success when measured in human standards.

All my life I have strived to be successful: to be a great athlete in high school and college, to get "outstanding" on my naval officer fitness reports, to be a "top gun" naval aviator, to be a tough resister in a Communist prison, to be commanding officer of an aircraft carrier, to rise to the top in military rank, to found a defense policy organization that would have an impact, and to establish a thriving small business in my retirement. When measured by human standards, I've succeeded in those areas—and I have been duly rewarded by athletic scholarships, early selection for service rank, military awards and decorations for my performance as a POW, choice duty assignments, and the praise of men.

However, those rewards have not been my greatest rewards. My experience as a POW in Vietnam helped me to see the difference between success as measured by men and success as seen in the eyes of God. There were many times in my lonely cell when my victories were known only by me and God, and I found that those victories were profoundly more rewarding than the times I received a pat on the back or a military award. Since my return to freedom, the opportunities I've had to share with others the love of God that sustained me during my captivity have been infinitely more precious than my chestful of military decorations. Writing my book, *Scars and Stripes*, as a testament to God's faithfulness during those dark days has brought satisfaction not paralleled by anything else.

And by far, the greatest rewards have come from times when I've done something simply because it was the right thing to do, when I've been criticized, or even ostracized, for taking an unpopular stand on causes which look like failures in the eyes of the world. Then, just as in my lonely cell, God knows and I know, and that is enough. My success has become significance.

THE FINAL SERMON

The last sermon I had prepared as prison chaplain in Hanoi was constructed out of the gloom and despair I felt about never being released. Strangely, God took me to the Book of Job, to the story of a man who had his share of trials and yet recovered. I never did deliver it in Hanoi because we were released just before the Sunday service. Instead, we held that service at Clark Air Force Base in the Philippines after we landed.

The words I prepared under the inspiration of God's Spirit while in captivity, took on new meaning and perhaps even more pertinence when I spoke them in freedom. This is the part of the sermon that stands out for me even now; I still think of it whenever I am tempted to ask the reason for what I endured. Job was a righteous and upright man who had great wealth, more than any other man in the land. He had seven sons and three daughters. He was a holy man who loved God, and God loved him. But Satan was able to come between the Lord and Job, so Job lost all his wealth, little by little. His house was blown down. He lost his seven sons and his three daughters. He was covered with boils, and all the people turned their backs on Job. This went on for a significant period of time.

But Job fell down on his knees and worshiped God and never once lost his integrity. He did not renounce his faith in God, but endured all that Satan could offer. God held him in highest esteem and returned to him what he had lost. God said, "My son, remember well these words I have spoken to you. As long as you live, you will be subject to change, whether you like it or not: now glad, now sorrowing; now vigorous, now lazy; now gloomy, now merry. Without battle, no man can come to victory; the greater the battle, the greater the victory.

Colonel Norman McDaniel
U.S. Air Force (Ret.) • Vietnam

Who am I? Why am I here? How should I live? Correct answers to these questions and a personal, positive response to them is the key to a successful and significant life.

First, I realize that I am a creation of the One, True, Almighty, and Everlasting God: the God of the Universe, and the Father of my Lord and Savior, Jesus Christ. I realize that through Christ, I have a personal, living relationship with God that is everlasting.

Second, I realize that my purpose in this mortal life is to establish and strengthen a personal relationship with God and to fulfill the unique purpose for which He created me.

Third, I should live by nurturing a right relationship with God by being a minister of His (in helping the poor, needy, sick, suffering, and those who do not know Him or have not accepted Him) and by doing all that I do to His glory. Also, I should live by giving my devotion and energy (in the following priority) to God, family, country, others, and self while sincerely trusting in the Holy Spirit to maintain the right balance and the right emphasis at the right time.

I accepted Jesus Christ as my Lord and Savior 15 years before I was shot down over North Vietnam and captured in 1966 during the Vietnam War. I spent almost seven years as a POW. During those long, endless years of torture, deprivation, and uncertainty, I was no stranger to God. I

148

prayed, trusted in Him, drew closer to Him during those trying, perilous times, and He sustained me.

My sincere advice to every person is found in the Bible, in Proverbs 3:5-6 which says, "Trust in the Lord with all thine heart; and lean not unto thine own understanding. In all thy ways acknowledge Him, and He shall direct thy paths."

I am persuaded that becoming aware of one's sinful condition, accepting Jesus Christ as your personal Savior, and then trusting in the Lord each day is the key to real and lasting significance!

KEEPING FAITH

The key to a meaningful life is knowing who you are, how you fit in the universe, and how to successfully meet the challenges of life. Those who are aware of this key and use it effectively are truly blessed. I learned early in life to operationalize Matthew 6:33, "Seek ye first the kingdom of God." Part of the operationalization is to be a man or woman of your word.

As an American POW in North Vietnam during the Vietnam War, I was tested many times on keeping faith in my country. During the winter of 1967, after being a POW for more than one and a half years, that faith was severely tested.

I was taken from my cell to an interrogation room. This interrogation was different from most of the previous ones. Usually it consisted of questions, threats, and torture, but never before the NVN POW Camp Commander. On this day, sitting beside the Camp Commander were his Chief Propaganda Officer and another lesser ranking military officer. The initial part of the interrogation was extremely friendly with the Camp Commander asking (through an interpreter) about my health and treatment. He proceeded to explain that the war was very tough for everyone with many people on both sides dying and being killed, it could last for many years and become much worse for me, and that I might never see my family again. When asked what I thought of his statement, I just acknowledged that I might never see my family again. Then he made an offer. He said, "But as for you, if you will help us, we will help you. We

149

can arrange for you to leave this prison camp and live in a neutral country, and your family can join you there. In that way, you can stay alive and be with your family again. All you have to do is write some letters, make some tapes, and make some appearances to help us win this war."

From a personal, selfish perspective, the offer was tempting. I could stay alive, I would not be tortured or worried about whether I'd live through the next moment, and I would be with my family again. However, from a professional, military warrior's perspective, the offer was a non-starter. In taking the oath as an Officer of the United States Air Force, I had sworn to support and defend the Constitution of the United States against all enemies, foreign and domestic, and that I would bear true faith and allegiance to the same. I was also committed to the U.S. Fighting Man's Code (Code of Conduct) that states in Article III, "I will accept neither parole nor special favors from the enemy."

The way the Vietnam War was going in 1967 with no end in sight, not accepting the Camp Commander's offer could have resulted in my dying (or being killed) while a prisoner and never seeing my family again. However, some things are worth dying for. For me, as an American POW in NVN, one of the things worth dying for was keeping faith with my country and fellow prisoners. This meant not collaborating with, aiding, or abetting the enemy to the extent that it would cause grave harm or death of my fellow prisoners, or cause me to return to my country feeling like, or being viewed as, a traitor. My answer to the Prison Camp Commander was, "I cannot accept your offer."

Some key guidance for a meaningful life is found in Psalms 15:4, "He that sweareth to his own hurt, and changeth not." This verse highlights the importance of being a man or woman of your word. That statement bears directly on integrity, loyalty, trust, and character.

As a POW I had an oath to keep, a Code of Conduct to follow, and a God to whom I must ultimately give an account for my life. Today, the last part of the previous sentence is still operative. If you haven't done so, I highly recommend that you also make it an operational part of your life.

NATIONAL POW-MIA RECOGNITION DAY

Until July 18, 1979, no commemoration was held to honor America's POW/MIAs, those who returned or those still missing and unaccounted for from our nation's wars. That first year, resolutions were passed in the Congress and a national ceremony was held at the National Cathedral, in Washington, D.C. The Missing Man formation was flown by the 1st Tactical Squadron, from Langley AFB, Virginia. The Veterans Administration published a poster including only the letters "POW/MIA" and that format was continued until 1982. At that time a black and white drawing of a POW in harsh captivity was created and used to convey the urgency of the situation. President Ronald Reagan assigned a high priority to achieving the fullest possible accounting for Americans still missing from the Vietnam War.

The National League of Families proposed the third Friday in September, a date not associated with any particular war and not in conjunction with any organization's national convention, as National POW/MIA Recognition Day. Ceremonies for this special day are now held throughout the nation and around the world on military installations, ships at sea, state capitols, at schools, churches, national veteran and civic organizations, police and fire departments, fire stations, etc. The League's POW/MIA flag is flown, and the focus is to ensure that America remembers its responsibility to stand behind those who served our nation and to do everything possible to account for those who do not return.

Captain J.B. McKamey
U.S. Navy (Ret.) • Vietnam

My advice for life can be summed up in these words: "the power of prayer." You may have a code to live by, or you may have a creed to operate under, but prayer will augment that code or creed. For help with advice for life, remember the words from the old hymn, "Take it to the Lord in prayer."

THE POWER OF PRAYER

My exposure to the power of prayer came early in my captivity in North Vietnam. I had been captured almost immediately after my parachute touched the ground. Evasion was out of the question with not a single tree within a mile for me to hide behind. I was captured and taken to the local prison, and the following day the interrogation began. My refusal to answer their questions led to beatings throughout the day, and this continued the following day. Near the end of the second day, the interrogator indicated that I was to be shot for refusing to cooperate. After a short note to my family, I began to pray. I did not pray for myself, but for my wife and children and others involved in the war. By the time the guard came for me, I had attained such serenity and peace of mind that I actually felt a let-down when I was told they had changed their mind. The interrogator also said my letter would be read over the radio. Realizing I had been tricked, I vowed to never believe anything I was told from that time on.

That experience made it easy to go to prayer for all things, large or small, from that time on. The power of prayer helped me through the rest of my captivity and has also been a source of inspiration since returning from Vietnam. The power of prayer can be summed up in these words, "Prayer is like preference cards. All reasonable requests will be fulfilled."

Willis Meier
WWII • ETO

Success in life is the result of honesty, integrity, caring, communication skills, leadership, knowledge, and expertise in our field of endeavor. Prepare for tomorrow, and being in the right place at the right time will take care of itself.

SACRED OBLIGATION

During WWII I served as an engineer/gunner on a B-24 Bomber crew with the 702nd Squadron, 445th Bomb Group, 2nd Air Division of the 8th Air Force. We were shot down on September 27, 1944, over Kassel, Germany. I was badly wounded, burned, and disabled, having bailed out at 28,000 feet, yet I survived three prison camps. When liberated by Russian troops, I weighed only 118 pounds. My survival was based upon my attitude and determination.

My daily prayer and the Lord's protection from the constant terrors, hardships, and starvation were my only means of coping. Many of my comrades were truly unrecognized heroes who paid a terrible price for serving their country. Therefore, we must continue to live up to America's sacred obligation to those who fought with honor and did not return home from many foreign battlefields. They deserve to never be forgotten.

Hiroshi Miyamura
Korea
Medal of Honor

As you and I know, our country has become great and has flourished because we are and have been a God-fearing nation. I hope that our youth today and the future generations to come will continue to believe in God and try to live with their fellow man. I truly believe that if the youth of today and our future generations would learn to judge a person by his or her actions and personality as an individual, then we will be a happier nation. I believe that learning of the Lord as a child helped me throughout my life, especially in the military while in Korea. For only God helped me through that night of April 24, 1951. I could not have survived without His guidance and protection.

CITATION

Cpl. Miyamura, a member of Company H, distinguished himself by conspicuous gallantry and intrepidity above and beyond the call of duty in action against the enemy. On the night of 24 April, Company H was occupying a defensive position when the enemy fanatically attacked threatening to overrun the position. Cpl. Miyamura, a machine gun squad leader, aware of the imminent danger to his men, unhesitatingly jumped from his shelter wielding his bayonet in close hand-to-hand combat killing approximately 10 of the enemy. Returning to his position, he administered first aid to the wounded and directed their evacuation. As another savage assault hit the line, he manned his machine gun and delivered withering fire until his ammunition was expended. He ordered the squad to withdraw while he stayed behind to render the gun inoperative. He then bayoneted his way through infiltrated enemy soldiers to a second gun emplacement and assisted in its operation.

When the intensity of the attack necessitated the withdrawal of the company, Cpl. Miyamura ordered his men to fall back while he remained to cover their movement. He killed more than 50 of the enemy before his ammunition was depleted and he was severely wounded. He maintained his magnificent stand despite his painful wounds, continuing to repel the attack until his position was overrun. When last seen, he was fighting ferociously against an overwhelming number of enemy soldiers.

Cpl. Miyamura's indomitable heroism and consummate devotion to duty reflect the utmost glory on himself and uphold the illustrious traditions on the military service.

Major Paul Montague
U.S. Marine Corps (Ret.) • Vietnam

Your past makes you what you are; never hide from the past. The best way to heal one's self is to talk about your experiences and not keep them within yourself. During my five years as a POW, I met Christ and Satan. I quickly learned that only with God in total control could I have peace within myself. Only then could I be a leader and an example to others.

ONE CHANCE OUT OF FOUR

I grew up on a farm; shortly after graduating from high school, I joined the Marine Corps. When my three-year enlistment was completed, I enrolled in college. I returned to the Marine Corps after I graduated from college and became a pilot. On my second tour in Vietnam, I was assigned to a mission supporting a flight of four Army helicopters. During the mission we were inserting troops on a landing zone west of Hue city.

On our first trip, two of the helicopters went down. One of the helicopters looked like it could be recovered so we flew back and got a pick-up crew who would try to recover the downed ship. Returning to the location of the landing zone and the downed helicopters, we inserted the crew. At the same time we came under heavy fire. The pick-up crew scrambled back into the helicopter and we took off. The gunfire was so heavy that the whole mountain west of us was lit up like a Christmas tree. When I got off the ground, we immediately began to lose power. I tried to use the radio, but it was dead and so was the control system. We rapidly lost power and altitude.

When we crashed I was apparently knocked unconscious. During this time I felt that I awoke and that I was in a black velvet box with no light. I thought, *Am I blind, dead or alive?* As I was trying to determine what had happened, a light with a peaceful face appeared. I had never seen the face before, but I trusted that it was alright. I questioned the face, "What are my chances of making it out of here?" In other words, I wanted to know what were my chances of surviving the crash and getting back to the base. The face answered, "One chance out of four." All I could think about was that those are really bad odds! By the time I realized that the face wasn't real, I began to regain consciousness.

I felt movement beside me and asked if it was my co-pilot; he responded, "Yes." I asked him if he had seen the light. As he wiggled to free himself from his seat, we realized that his seat had been torn loose and apparently flew across the aircraft landing on my seat. If I had not been thrown from my seat, the weight of the co-pilot and his seat would have killed me. Not being crushed by the co-pilot and his seat made me believe that I had been spared by the hand of God.

The only way for us to get out of the helicopter was between the rudder pedals on the floor and the plexiglass panels. Before I was able to free myself from the aircraft, I saw six North Vietnamese soldiers waiting for us. This was the beginning of my four years and eleven months as a prisoner of war.

The third time I was tortured (the torture lasted for over one month) I was forced to remain in a kneeling position on concrete with my arms tied over my head in the door of my cell. Late at night I saw someone walking down the path carrying a lantern. When he reached the door of my cell, he set the lantern on the step in front of me and said, "Go ahead and pray to your God, but he can't help you!" With that I raised my eyes and found myself looking into the eyes of Satan. When he left, I told God that if He would help me, I would be His the rest of my life.

After a period of time the guard and the political officer came to get me for an interview They took me from my cell and had me sit on a stool. The political officer started the interrogation asking, "Do you want to go home?" I responded, "Yes, I want to go home." He then asked why I wanted to go home. I told him, "I want to see my poor aging mother, my poor wife, and my three little children." They then asked what I would do if I went home. I answered again, "I will go to see my poor aging mother, my wife, and my three little children."

At that time, they began to talk to each other, and one of the inter-rogators asked if I had ever been tortured? I responded, "Yes" and said, "Twice by him," pointing at the political officer. With my response, they turned to the political officer. After more time passed, the political officer left, returning with a confession for me to sign. The confession said that I had tried to escape and I had an escape plan. I refused to sign the confession, telling them it was untrue. They asked why I wouldn't sign the confession, and I explained that I told them I had attempted to escape only to stop the torture.

Frustrated, the political officer took me to another room with a stool, a small desk with an ink pen, and paper on the desktop. He told me to sit down and write why I wanted to go home. I wrote, "I want to go home to see my poor aging mother, my poor wife, and my three little children." He took the paper, read it, and then handed it back and asked, "What will you do if you go home?"

I wrote again, "I will go see my poor aging mother, my poor wife, and my three little children."

Taking the paper and reading again, frustrated, he replied, "Just write if you will ever come back to Vietnam!" I told him, "I will go anywhere my Government sends me." I know that God gave me the courage to respond with that statement because I wasn't brave enough to respond like that on my own. The political officer began to cry as he and the guard took me back to my cell.

It was then that I realized that God had defeated Satan. God gave me the strength and the knowledge to survive my time as a prisoner of war. He still guides me today. It was ten years before God revealed to me the meaning of the statement, "You have one chance out of four." The meaning: Who are you going to obey? Satan? Someone else? Yourself? Or God? The first three responses are all forms of Satan. The only chance you have is to listen to and obey God.

Mark Moore
WWII • ETO

I was a nine-year-old child when, at an altar in a small church in Houston, Texas, I made a commitment to live for Christ. Later I discovered two short words that have been important guides in my decisions and actions.

One word is BE. This challenged me to "BE all that you can be!" I would not allow my actions, though sometimes short of my goals, to discourage me. "You can BE better than that," became a constant reminder.

The other word is DO. I cannot recall when I adopted the philosophy, "DO what you can, with what you have, where you are." However, these two attitudes have been faithful guides for me over many years.

THE PRAYER OF A SMALL BOY

After I completed Chaplain School on May 8, 1944, I was assigned to the 106th Division stationed at Camp Atterbury, Indiana. In September we began our move to England. On November 25, 1944, with black blinds on the windows, I knelt at the altar of a small base chapel in Gloucester, England. As I read the Psalms by the light that flickered from the fire in a small stove nearby, a portion of Scripture caught my attention. It was Psalm 66 that reads: "For you, O God, tested us. You refined us like silver. You brought us into prison and laid burdens on our backs. You let men ride over our heads; we went through fire and water, but You brought us out into a place of abundance" (NIVS). I was so impressed that I wrote on the flyleaf of the New Testament, the reference, the date, time, and the words, "God's promise to me."

We were moved to Europe and up to the front lines of the battle replacing the war-tested Second Division. We were told that this was a rest area and that we would begin to get some combat experience here. However, on December 16, 1944, the Battle of the Bulge began. I was stationed at St. Vith, several miles behind the front lines. General Leo McMann, Commander of the 106th Division, wanted a Chaplain to go to the front to be with the artillery units supporting the two Infantry Regiments, the 422nd and the 423rd. I was selected.

I worked in the Aid Station praying with the wounded and endeavoring to comfort the dying. Rather than returning to St. Vith for the night, I stayed with the men on the front. By morning I saw the wisdom in staying with these forward units. The battle raged many days and nights. I was captured on December 19, 1944, at a time when we were completely surrounded and there was no hope of escape.

About 3,000 of us prisoners were being moved to Bad Orb in boxcars when we were attacked and bombed by RAF planes whose target was the Limburg railroad yard. Needless to say, we were all praying and hoping that the bombs would miss their target. My wife, Clarice, had written me many letters, some of which were returned to her. Among those returned was one letter that told a story about our son, Kent. Apparently while at church, he was tired and wanted to go to sleep. Before he laid his head in her lap he prayed, "Father bless and keep my Daddy and bring him home to me and Mommy." When I returned home, as best as we could place the time of his prayer, it was at the same time that we were being bombed. I believe the prayer of a small boy, and no doubt many others, reached the ears of God and spared us great tragedy.

We were bombed again on April 5, 1945, at the Nuremberg, Germany, railroad yards. I was put in charge of helping bind the wounds of those injured and also had to help with the identification of 24 American officers who were killed. Although a difficult assignment, it was a sacred privilege to secure one dog tag to the body and take the other, plus small personal belongings such as a billfold, watch, or ring and put them together in one of their socks to be delivered to the next of kin.

Near Gars on the Inns River we were liberated by the 86th Infantry Division. I asked one of the liberators if he knew my brother who was in the 86th. Captain Barney Slagle, a Forward Observer with the Artillery, helped me find my brother's room. We had a glorious reunion.

After a week I went to Camp Lucky Strike and on to New York. Truly God kept His promise for, "He brought us into a wealthy place." I have learned to "Do what you can, with what you have, where you are." Trust in our gracious God to be faithful. He will do whatever seems wise unto Him.

TAP CODE USED IN VIETNAM "SMITTY HARRIS TAP CODE"

Taps	1	2	3	4	5
1	A	B	C	D	E
2	F	G	H	I	J
3	L	M	N	O	P
4	Q	R	S	T	U
5	V	W	X	Y	Z

The letter K is dropped from the alphabet and
the letter C is substituted. The letter X is used between
sentences. Each letter is tapped out by its position on the grid.
The horizontal position is tapped first, followed by
the vertical position. For example:

A = tap...tap.
B = tap...tap, tap.
F = tap, tap...tap.

G = tap, tap...tap, tap
B = tap...tap, tap.
U = tap, tap, tap, tap...tap, tap, tap, tap, tap.
GBU = God Bless U

Colonel Herschel "Scotty" Morgan
U.S. Air Force (Ret.) • Vietnam

I have found that a leader communicates what he expects, then gives his people the tools and the breathing room to get the job done. Finally, he gives his people credit for what they have done and rewards them with praise and promotions. Action, not words, gets the job done.

GIVE ME WISDOM

On April 3, 1965, I was shot down over North Vietnam and captured two days later. During the next 2,872 days, I learned many things about myself and also many valuable lessons. The first is the value of freedom. The key to surviving those difficult and sometimes brutal circumstances was faith in God, my country, my fellow POWs, and myself. I gained this faith throughout my life by osmosis—by soaking up the values taught by parents, family, church, school, Sunday school teachers, scout leaders, and those special people that we all have in our lives. We find that when we have nothing else, faith sustains us!

I learned not to worry about those things over which I had no control. I learned to pray not, "Why did you do this to me, Lord?" but I learned to ask God to give me the wisdom to know what is right and the strength to do right even when no one is watching.

William "Sonny" Mottern
WWII • ETO
Past National Commander
American Ex-POW Association 1996-1997

During WWII, U.S. troops were the best equipped fighting men in the world. But the one vital element that enabled me to survive the war and POW camp was not GI issue. It was supplied by my father and mother. It was portable, took no space in my barracks bag, and being invisible, could not be confiscated by the enemy. It was my faith—my Christian upbringing. My faith became a mighty bulwark against the brutality, cold, hunger, forced marches, boxcar rides, and bombing I endured. Faith became my constant companion, my comfort against the inhumanity of my enemy. I did not have to return it to the quartermaster when I was discharged. I brought it back home with me and relied on it to help raise my family, run a successful business, and to return to society some of the good fortune that has come my way through faith.

THE CHICKEN AND THE EGG

In April 1945, I was one of over 10,000 POWs who were forced to march from Nuremberg to Moosberg, Germany. The guards at that time were older soldiers, too old to do anything else except to lead us to Moosberg. One day I saw a barn about 100 yards from the column. Being an old hillbilly from the country, I thought to myself. "Where there is a barn, there must be some hay; and if there is hay, there could be a chicken; and that chicken just might be on a nest laying an egg!" Looking around to make sure I was not being watched, I dashed to the barn.

Once inside the barn, I noticed a ladder leading to the loft. I climbed to the loft and sure enough, there in the corner was a chicken on a nest. I was raised on a farm in Tennessee, and I knew the difference between a setting hen and a laying hen. A setting hen has a low profile and looks straight ahead, while a laying hen sits high on the nest and is always on the lookout for trouble.

I thought to myself, "If I try to grab the chicken and it flies through my arms, I will lose both the chicken and the egg." I waited to make sure that she had already laid an egg, then I made my move. I grabbed for the chicken, already thinking of a chicken and egg meal. Sure enough, she flew right between my arms. I missed the chicken but I did get the egg. I was so hungry that I cracked that egg immediately and sucked it dry. That was my meal for the day. I learned a lesson that day about greed and selfishness; neither pays much of a dividend in life. I sometimes share this story with elementary school students in an attempt to teach them that greed and selfishness don't pay. Occasionally I will meet these students after they are out of school, and they will reflect on the story about greed, the chicken and the egg.

I have come to the conclusion that you have to have faith in God and that you have to trust Him. I would like to encourage everyone to take a few minutes to evaluate how your life is going and ask yourselves if the Spirit of God is at work in your life. You will find that life lived here and now is lived better as a child of God. There is no question what a difference it will make in your eternity. There are many who have no real hope beyond life on earth. The best they can hope for is that there is no life after death. The worst will be to find out that the message of the Bible is true and that there is a heaven and there is a hell, but for them, there is no hope for heaven. That's bad news of the worst kind. There is no reason for anyone to live without hope. Accept Jesus Christ as your Lord and Savior and receive a spirit of power and love, self-discipline, and the hope of being in the presence of God forever. When a person is right with God, by His grace, they can know that life never ends! (Titus 3:7)

Timon Mouser
WWII • Germany

My advice for life is: Always be honest. My generation grew up believing that your word is your bond. As a soldier, I found out that physical courage is important, but moral courage is harder to obtain and more important. I also believe that it is important to have faith in God and to trust Him.

A GREAT HOMECOMING

In 1943 I entered the Army a scared young boy, but I came home a man. I was assigned to the 298th Combat Engineers. We landed on Omaha Beach on D-Day plus one. I was captured during the battle for Saint-Lo in France. I was a prisoner of war at Stalag IIIB until the camp was liberated by the Russians. After the liberation, I walked all the way to Warsaw before I was able to join American troops, was then moved to Naples, Italy, and finally to the United States and Boston. I made my way back to Missouri. My family was a farming family and had no telephone so they did not even know that I was coming home. When I walked into the house, it was a complete surprise...what a great homecoming!

The Lord was with me. I know it is because of Him that I returned home, and I am blessed to have lived through the experience. I am a Sunday school leader in my church. Thank you, Lord!

Captain James Mulligan
U.S. Navy (Ret.) • Vietnam

I learned the importance of all human companionship while kept in solitary confinement for more than three and one half years. I could remember nothing bad about anyone I had ever known and would have given anything to have just one of them with me.

In my life the word commitment is the operative word for all those things I believe in: marriage, family, God, country, etc. You make a commitment to what you believe in, and you stand by that commitment.

The word "persistence" is my guideline to reach goals and objectives. Be persistent and never, ever give up, and eventually you will achieve what you are seeking. Remember that with God all things are possible! So learn to pray!

I was a POW for seven years in North Vietnam. During that period, I spent more than 42 months in solitary confinement, in a closet with three walls and a door. This experience left me with time to think about who I was and what I really believed in. I asked myself many questions, among them, "What are my real religious beliefs? What is my civic responsibility in American society?" I also asked, "What is important in becoming a good American? What should every American child learn in order to become a good citizen, and where should they obtain this information?"

After much reflection, I concluded that the United States is the product of western civilization and Judeo-Christian traditions, molded by the Age of Enlightenment. At that point I decided that if we were going to teach our children to be good Americans, we would have to do the following:

1. Our children need to read, study, understand, and live by the Ten Commandments.

2. Our children also need to read, study, understand, and live by the principles taught in the message from the Sermon on the Mount.

3. Our children need to read, study, understand, and live by the Constitution of the United States and the Bill of Rights.

The rules of behavior set for us in these documents are the foundation of our democratic republic. Collectively, they signify what American citizens are all about. If all of us follow what they prescribe, we will never confuse true freedom with crass permissiveness.

Further, I believe that these concepts apply equally to Americans of all religions, races, colors, and nationalities. These concepts, these tenets, are the glue that holds all of us together in this great American experiment. They are what make us one nation under God, allowing us to experience liberty and justice for all.

Our children must understand that the freedoms we enjoy as American citizens were never freely given but were obtained with blood, sweat, tears, pain, and loss of life. They have to understand that for every right and every privilege they enjoy, they have a corresponding obligation and duty.

Every generation of Americans must understand that our democratic republic with its representative government is a fragile system. It must be nurtured and the founding principles have to be respected. Without any of these we are doomed to return to either tyranny or anarchical slavery, and the noble experiment will have failed. The choice falls upon every American. There is a burden to carry and every citizen must share it equally.

THE LIFELINE

In May 1968, the summer heat was terrible. I was in a cell in the part of Hanoi Hilton that we called Alcatraz. My cell was terribly, terribly hot. I would estimate the temperature to be around 130 degrees. I was so hot and so miserable that it was very difficult to even breathe. To get fresh air, I would get down on the floor and try to suck air from below the door. The sun would come up and beat down on the door of my cell. Covering my door was a large iron plate, and that iron plate would become terribly hot to the point where I felt like I was going out of my mind because of the heat. I couldn't eat anything; I couldn't sleep. I was dying because of the oppressive heat and finally got to the point where I couldn't stand it anymore. It was night and I began to pray, "Lord, Lord, you've got to do something. You've got to help me. You've got to do something; I can't stand it. I'm at the end...I can't go on anymore." I was begging for mercy, and I heard this faint rumble off in the distance, and all of a sudden, another rumble and then some loud rumbles, followed by tremendous thunder and lightning. A massive thunderstorm came in and inundated the camp with water. Lightning was crackling all over the place, and the water came up so high, that it came under the door of my cell and it cooled off the cell. I said to myself, "You know, when you get back...you're going to say, 'that was just a cold front going through.'" But deep in my heart, I knew it was the good Lord answering my prayers. At the very moment, when I couldn't take it any longer, God answered my prayer. I believe it is one of life's spiritual lessons that I learned in Hanoi. The Lord lets you get to a point where you have to call on and depend only on Him. Then He throws you a lifeline when you least expect it and probably when you need it the most. It's then that you are willing to acknowledge God, and you realize the importance of the spiritual aspect of life.

THE PLEDGE OF ALLEGIANCE

I pledge allegiance to the flag

of the United States of America

and to the Republic for which it stands,

one nation, under God, indivisible

with liberty and justice for all.

Grover Mullins
WWII • Germany

I think one of most important character qualities is to never give up. I am alive today because my crew never gave up even when the situation seemed hopeless. I also believe everyone should try to be honest; and for me, personally, hard work and persistence have always been important.

A STROKE OF LUCK OR THE HAND OF GOD?

I was born in the small town of Houstonia, Missouri, on July 31, 1920. When I was very young we moved to the Ozarks, and I grew up in Lebanon, Missouri. During WWII, I was a flight engineer on a B-17 Bomber with the 8th Air Force. We were shot down January 11, 1944 over Oscheraleben, Germany. I was a POW in Stalag XVII in Linz, Austria.

My eighth mission was the Bremen Raid. We were flying a daylight bombing mission in a B-17 named the Stardust. The temperature outside the aircraft was 67 degrees below zero, one of the coldest days recorded. Flying in winter at high altitudes is dangerous at best, and disaster can come quickly.

Three German fighters attacked us just as we started our bombing run. We were hit in the nose section, and the nose of the B-17 was shot away. The 20-mm fire from the fighters blew out the plexiglass in the nose of the plane, destroyed half of our available oxygen, knocked out one engine, destroyed our communication system, and left a large hole in the wing. The gunfire had killed the navigators, and the wind coming through the open nose of the plane blew away all the navigator's maps.

The temperature alone was deadly, but an aircraft with an open nose, complicated with gale force winds, airspeed, and sub-zero temperatures spelled doom for the crew. We were unable to remain with our formation, but the pilot managed to maneuver the B-17 into another group of planes flying over the target. The bombardier was, however, unconscious, wounded, and gasping for air because his face mask had been torn away.

The situation was desperate. I worked to drop the bomb load but was only able to get about two-thirds of them to fall. We remained a flying bomb. I ran back and forth between the injured bombardier, whose face was swollen to the size of a basketball, and the pilot, carrying bottles of oxygen so he would not pass out. I frequently had to return to the top turret position to make sure there were no enemy aircraft.

We continued to fall farther and farther behind the formation and soon found ourselves alone over the English Channel in a crippled aircraft. It seemed all hope was lost, but then a stroke of luck or the providential hand of God intervened. Off in the distance we saw a lone airplane on a search-and-rescue mission over the channel. Our lives saved, we followed that plane back to a British airdrome.

William Murray
WWII • ETO

On January 6, 1922, I was born into a religious family that had faith in God and tried to do things the Lord's way. During the 30s, due to drought, dust storms, and the Depression, my family's faith was put to the test!

I joined the Army Air Corps as a private in September 1942. In April 1944, on my 14th bombing raid over Germany, I was shot down and taken a prisoner of war for 13 months. My faith was extremely tested, not knowing what was in the future.

I had married Norma Jean Montgomery in May 1942, just before I joined the Army. Over the years, our faith and love have grown. I believe faith in God is what gives a person a meaningful and successful life.

GOD'S LOVING, WATCHFUL CARE

God was looking out for me from the day that I was born. I weighed five pounds and had double pneumonia and was carried around on a pillow, yet I managed to survive. I am sure that there were many prayers that were offered for me. My mother died when I was only eight, and life was not easy.

During World War II, I was stationed in England and was a ball turret gunner on a B-17. On my eighth raid over Europe, the plane was flying through heavy flak, some of which broke the plexiglass and gears in the ball turret on the underside of the plane. Some of the plexiglass and metal fragments cut my face and injured my eyes. As the door of the turret opened, the prop blasted more of the fragments into my eyes, temporarily blinding me. Amazingly, after a short stay in the hospital. I was released with no permanent damage.

On our 14th raid we were shot down. It was a beautiful, clear and quiet day, so our B-17 and our parachutes were highly visible. My chute was smaller than the others because it had to fit in the cramped space in the ball turret. Because of the smaller parachute, I fell faster and away from the other men in my crew.

When I landed, a young woman and a young girl who spoke English took my money and told me to walk with them. They were trying to help me escape by taking me to the Underground. We passed one German soldier, but the second soldier realized I was an American, so the lady told him that they were turning me in. I was taken to City Hall and sat in a corner on the floor while the people of the community filed past shaking their fist and yelling at me. We had been told that some American airmen were being executed by hanging, so I was extremely uneasy.

The next morning a member of the Gestapo took me on a motorcycle with a sidecar to join the rest of my crew. When we passed the Black Forest, the soldier offered to let me make a run for it, but I was convinced that he would shoot me in the back, so I declined.

After the interrogation, we were loaded in a boxcar that was 40x8 feet in dimension. We were unable to sit down due to lack of room and we had nothing to eat and very little water. We did not get out of the boxcar for three days and two nights.

We arrived in the POW camp in pretty rough shape after the long ride. As we walked up the hill to the prison camp, the Austrian people threw rocks at us.

Living conditions in the camp were very poor. We slept eight men to a bunk on a mattress made of straw that was infested with lice. We ended up burning the mattresses. The camp was also infested with fleas, other bugs, and rodents. The showers were located up the hill in a building where the Germans were quartered. We had three showers in the 13 months we were there. Each time we were allowed to shower, our heads were shaved. According to the Geneva Convention, we were to receive three hot meals a day. We did receive three hot meals, but two of them were only hot water.

The war ended on May 8, 1945. Most of the American prisoners were marched out of the camp in April. I had to remain because my right leg was paralyzed. In all, 110 of us were unable to walk, so were left behind. On May 12, Russian troops entered the camp and offered to take the remaining Americans back to Russia. No one accepted the offer and the next day General Patton's 11th Armored Division arrived and took us to the American line in Linz, Austria.

My brother Roger was with the 11th Armored Division and when I inquired about him, I found out that he was away looking for me in some of the other POW camps in the same area. We were moved to the airfield waiting to get on a plane bound for either Paris or England. I waited until they were loading the very last plane. There was not enough room for all of us, and five men would have to remain behind three days before they could fly out. I volunteered to stay because I knew my brother was looking for me. At the same time, Roger heard that I was at the airport in the process of flying out to England or France. As the last plane took off down the runway, he came driving his jeep across the railroad bridge. That was one time that volunteering paid off, because I was able to be with him. We had three days together before I had to leave for a hospital in Paris for a six-week stay to help partially regain the weight that I had lost.

During my time as a prisoner of war, I was able to read the New Testament four times. I learned that difficult times can be a blessing in disguise as we begin to see God working in our lives when He fulfills our hopes and calms our fears. I would never want to go through the experience again, but it was worth it because our efforts ensured freedom for future generations. I know that I would have never survived all that happened to me without God's loving and watchful care.

William Paschal
WWII • ETO

The experiences in prison camp profoundly affected and strengthened my belief in a power greater than man. I entered the Army at the age of 17, was trained, entered combat, and was imprisoned in short order. I was released from prison camp in Germany six months before my 20th birthday. As a young man, I did not have a deep faith or religious feelings, but I attended church, worshiped, and did the religious thing, because it was the norm for our family and our community. "Non-committed" would best describe the depth of my faith and feelings at the time.

I came out of prison camp convinced that God is everywhere at all times and is to be found by every living person as we reach out to accept His help. I was awakened by a strong vibrant voice speaking out in the black of night, speaking of hope when despair and hopelessness engulfed an entire prison of American POWs in Germany. We regained the power to endure and to live for tomorrow. The experience brought peace of mind and endless hope to those who had once despaired of hope and thought their life would soon be over. This lesson of life has stayed with me to this day.

THE SINGER

Things looked pretty grim at Stalag IXB, Bad Orb, Germany. When our column of prisoners of war marched up to the gate on February, 14, 1945, we could tell by looking at the prisoners inside the wire that this was not a happy place. They all looked gaunt and unkempt. One of the German-speaking prisoners in our group asked the guard at the gate, "What kind of camp is this?" The guard replied in a short, brusque manner. The American prisoner did not respond when his comrades asked what the guard said. Later the word got around that the guard had replied that we would all be dead from disease or starvation within six months.

Our group had been captured during the German offensive, "Nordwind," the sequel to the Battle of the Bulge. This operation started at midnight, December 31, 1944. Our tanks had been sent northward to break the stranglehold around Bastogne. Our infantry group had been mauled and literally chewed up by the Tiger tanks, moving almost unopposed through our position outside Rimling, France. Those of us who survived, surrendered on the morning of January 8, 1944. We had been cut off from our lines of supply for two days. Seven of us found ourselves, not just surrounded, but also out of ammunition, food, and water.

When we arrived at the gate of the POW camp, we had taken only one shower since leaving the States in October. I had only shaved twice in that time and had no haircut for the past 90 days. We thought we looked bad, but the guys that were already in the camp looked worse! Most of them had been captured around December 16th, during the Battle of the Bulge.

The camp barracks were stone for the first three feet, then a single layer of board the rest of the way. In our barracks, there was ice on the inside of the boards every morning from the condensation of the breath of the prisoners. There was no overnight fire allowed in the stove, so we froze at night. When it snowed, snow always found its way inside near the spot on the floor where I slept. We slept on burlap bags filled with wood shavings. Everyone soon contracted lice from these burlap bags. Even though it was the coldest winter of record in European history, the prisoners would take their pants, shirts, and underwear off during the day and smash lice.

Our morning meal was soup that was made from green turnip tops, sugar beet tops, or grass. This meal always gave us an almost immediate relief from constipation. Morning coffee (in name only) was made by boiling acorns or bark. The latrines outside were slit trenches with a log alongside. At night 300 men were locked in the barracks with a single, one-hole toilet and one water faucet. Toilet paper was unheard of. Diarrhea and dysentery were rampant. At night we shared a loaf of bread and about three boiled potatoes or a cup of turnip or rutabaga soup among six men. As the number of prisoners increased, we shared the same rations among eight men. The recipe for bread allowed for 20% tree flour or sawdust, sugar beet tops, and a small amount of rye.

During the day, we passed our time doing nothing—there was no recreation or reading material. At 5:00 PM each day we were locked into our barracks to endure another night, only to awaken to the same thing each morning. Within 10 days all of us newcomers could tell we were losing weight. When we arrived, our gear was taken from us. We had no canteen, cup, utensils, or mess kit. I ate and washed out of my helmet. I was able to carve a crude spoon from a small piece of wood.

Initially our talk was centered around *when* we would be liberated. After a few weeks, the talk centered around *if* we would be liberated. Some of the prisoners who were captured earlier began to die of malnutrition and typhus or similar diseases. Some of the men disassociated themselves from the rest of the group; they wouldn't talk; they stayed in bed and slept away the day and the night. They were the first to die. Over time, the attitude of the prisoners became pessimistic about the future.

One evening in early February, after we were locked in the barracks, I heard a strong voice from the dark, saying, "I will recite to you the 23rd Psalm," and proceeded to do so. Some of the men made catcalls and booed. I then heard the same strong voice begin singing hymns, first *Onward Christian Soldier*, then *In the Garden*, and *Softly and Tenderly*, followed by others. As he continued, the dissenting outcries stopped and were silent. Every night after that, night after night, I could hear that strong voice quoting Scripture from the New Testament. The soldier told us that if we believed in a higher power, we could endure, and we could make it. He exhorted us not to forsake compassion, not to give up hope, not to withdraw from life, and then he would lead the group in songs and discussion. I spent a number of days trying to find out who it was that had this strong voice that offered us so much comfort. I eventually met him. His name was Glen Schmidt, and he was a soldier from the 42nd Division. On February 22, I was one of 89 prisoners selected and sent to another labor camp near Leipzig. Liberation followed, and I returned to my life as a civilian, went to school, married, had children, and pursued a career. Periodically I wondered about the men that I had known in prison, including Glen Schmidt. Glen had made a strong impression on everybody. I am convinced that many men are alive today because he brought faith, hope, and sanity to an otherwise insane and brutal environment.

In the mid 1990s, I began to attend reunions of my Infantry Division and survivors of Stalag IXB. We attended a reunion at the Holiday Inn, in Tucson, Arizona. After checking in, Marjorie, my wife, and I went to the hospitality room. When I entered the room I heard a strong and familiar voice. I walked over to the man, moved in front of him and said, "Hello, Glen Schmidt! I have always wondered if you survived the camps." Glen was showing people in the group an Army helmet with a bullet hole in it. Apparently, he and his teenage son had visited the Maginot line area in France, where he had been captured after a bullet shot had ripped off his helmet. His son found the helmet at the very spot where Glen was captured. During our conversation, I mentioned that I was a retired dentist living in Wichita, Kansas. An odd look came on Glen's face. He said, "In 1969, I retired from the Air Force at McConnell Air Force base in Wichita, Kansas." God works in strange ways...all those years and our paths had never crossed.

Walter Pawlesh
WWII • ETO
Past National Commander
American Ex-POW Association 1973-1974

Faith must be the most important part of our lives. In the Scriptures we are told, "Without faith it is impossible to please Him."

HEAVEN CAN WAIT

I feel we must always play the cards in life that God has dealt us. I may not know where my mission in life will take me or what God wants me to do, but I must try to make the right decisions. My faith is my main guide through life.

While I was a tail gunner on a B-17 Flying Fortress Bomber, I had a pattern that I followed before each mission. When the pilot would release the brakes of the plane, I would start saying the "Lord's Prayer," and I had to complete it before we lifted off the runway. The name of our bomber was "Heaven Can Wait," and it always lived up to its name as it brought our crew of ten men back safely from the war. We were shot down and crash-landed, but all of the crew were alive.

I remember a story a POW friend of mine related to me. He would go to visit the Chaplain to receive his blessing before each mission. Once he asked the Chaplain, "Don't you think the German military men are visiting their chaplains too? So, whose side is God on?" We knew He was with us during the war. But at the time we may have wondered what God wanted us to do.

Alvar Platt
WWII • ETO

As you pursue your education, you will eventually be offered two possibilities about the origin of life.

1. There was a big bang millions of years ago, and following that, the process of evolution developed, and here we are. Those who adhere to this persuasion don't know what caused the big bang, and there are a myriad of other things missing besides the link. In spite of these difficulties, this is what is taught today in school as science.

2. The other premise is that there is a Divine Creator that put all these things together and created us. He came down to earth in bodily form and paid a ransom for us that we couldn't pay so that we might spend eternity with Him. You can read all about this in a book that is still a bestseller.

My advice for life is: Read the Book. I once heard Pastor E.V. Hill say, "I don't want to go to hell; there ain't no exits!" There are instructions in the Book on how to avoid going to hell. Some say BIBLE stands for "Basic Instructions Before Leaving Earth."

"MAYDAY" ON A MAY DAY

May 1, 1943, started out like any other day that we were alerted for a mission. We got up for breakfast, briefing and assembling our guns. I was a waist gunner—the position was the coldest spot on the plane. With both windows open and flying at a couple hundred miles per hour, there was always a nice breeze. On this day we had mechanical problems with our plane, and we figured we were going to miss the mission. There was another plane ready to go, but one of the officers was sick, so we took over their ship. We didn't even have time to change to our guns.

New groups were arriving daily and, as was customary, a new pilot would ride along as co-pilot with seasoned crews to get an idea of what they would be getting into before they took the full responsibility. Major Rosener, a commanding officer of a new group would be flying with us as co-pilot. The target was one we had been to several times before in the 16 missions we had flown, so we weren't expecting any surprises. To hit the submarine pens on the French coast, we approached the target from land so the bombardier would have something to line his sights on. As we approached the target, the bombardier actually flew the plane using the bomb sights.

After we dropped our bombs, we turned and headed back out to sea, dropping down to a lower altitude below the enemy radar. Major Rosener came back through the waist, and I asked him how he liked the mission. Up until that point, it had been an easy one. He responded that he didn't think he would have any trouble making 25 like this one. He would change his mind before the day was over, for 30 minutes later we were talking in a dinghy.

Flying back we had to penetrate a broken cloud formation at about 6,000 feet and the group split up going through the clouds. We were at about 1,000 feet and the visibility was poor. We were flying in a diamond formation with several other planes. After leaving Saint-Nazaire, we encountered strong winds from the northwest that had blown us back toward the French coast. We were still flying in a fairly heavy cloud cover when land was sighted. We hoped it was England, but when I got a glimpse of it, I recognized it immediately as Brest, France. Using the intercom I called the pilot and informed him the land we had spotted was not England, but France, and it might be a good idea to get into a better

189

formation. Before we were able to do so, we were attacked head-on by a group of German FW 190s, and we took several hits. We lost our pilot and one engine with the first pass and fell out of formation. When you get out of formation you receive lots of attention.

The German fighters began making numerous passes at us from both directions. We were hit again. When I looked over I saw that the right waist gunner had taken a direct hit and must have been killed instantly. I decided to put on my parachute, and, as I bent over to pick it up, it was blown out of my hand. I received shrapnel injures in my legs, and also was hit by what I thought was a 30-caliber bullet on the outside of my right thigh exiting on the inside. I immediately sat down on an ammunition box, and in just moments, we hit water, and I mean HIT!

We had rehearsed ditching procedures on a regular basis. However, our problem was that we didn't know that we were going to hit water. The plane was on fire, and the smoke was so heavy in the cockpit that Major Rosener couldn't even see out. The wind that had blown us off course was creating swells that appeared to be about 40 feet high, making ditching a hazardous operation at best. The left wing of the plane must have hit first because it was folded back against the fuselage, blocking the window when I tried to get out. The fuselage broke behind the radio room and initially let in enough water to provide a cushion for me. I was immediately under water in a lot of debris. I could see light at the waist window, which I swam to, but it was blocked by the wing and I couldn't budge it. I have always been able to hold my breath for quite a while, but I was beginning to wonder when and where I was going to get my next one. Just then a large wave caught the wing and pulled it away from the window, and I was able to swim out and inflate my Mae West life jacket. As I came to the surface, I saw the tail of the ship sinking out of sight along with half the crew.

No one had had time to release the dinghies. One of them had been thrown out on impact, but it was so full of small shrapnel holes that we had to pump it continually to keep it inflated enough to keep the five of us together. When it would float to the top of a swell, the white cap on top of the swell would drench us. We took turns pumping for the rest of the afternoon, on into the night, and during the next day. We were eventually picked up by a French fishing boat with two German officers on board and landed at Saint-Malo, France. We were taken to an army camp, given first aid and some food. I was then moved to a hospital for treatment of my wounds and eventually moved by train to Germany to begin my time in a POW camp.

As Paul Harvey might say, now for the rest of the story. My father was a preacher in California, and he prayed for me every day. On the day we were shot down, my father was going from his home in Ripon to his church in Manteca. He usually waited to get to church to pray for me, but on this day, he felt a profound need to pray for me; it was an urgent need so strong that he pulled his car off the road and prayed. I'm thankful that he realized the urgency of the situation because I could not have held my breath until he got to his office in Manteca. Neither of us felt this was a coincidence when we later compared our notes and checked the dates and the time. We realized that his urgent prayer was offered at the same time that we crashed. Coincidence, I don't think so...the story is similar to the story of the nobleman in John 4:46-53, "So the father knew that it was at the same hour, in which Jesus said unto him, Thy son liveth...."

John Playter
WWII • PTO

At a very early age, I learned from my father to be honest and trust-
worthy. Dad was only seen at church during weddings or funerals, but his
example depicted Christian principles. Mom was the churchgoer, and I
went with her. The importance of Bible study was prominent in her life,
and this led to my profession of faith at the age of fourteen. Although not
being as good and as fervent a student of the Bible as I should have been,
I learned, and have never forgotten, the Lord's Prayer. I recognized and
have always tried to practice what is said in Matthew 6:33: "But, seek ye
first the kingdom of God, and his righteousness; and all these things shall
be added unto you."

ANSWERED PRAYER

I was overseas when World War II began. I soon realized that I was serving a nation that was not prepared for war, and I was serving with troops sorely disappointed with our nation. Lack of materiel and lack of food and medicine soon took its toll, and after only four months of no allied assistance, we became prisoners of ruthless captors who placed little value on human life. Forced to work with little food and medicine, I survived two years and five months. Daily prayers for strength and hope were raised. But the daily indignities by our captors and even a forced affront to my loyalty to America, tended to make prayer seem futile. A forced loading onto a "Hellship" brought a change. Seventeen days, yet traveling only a very short distance, brought direct hits by two American-fired torpedoes. This freed 82 of us but brought death to 668.

At the request of a fellow prisoner, I traded locations with him less than two minutes before the torpedoes struck. I survived; he didn't. For 60 years I wondered why I survived but other God-fearing men hadn't. The only explanation has to be answered prayer. Fear of, but trusting God, is required of us all.

Captain Charles Plumb
U.S. Navy (Ret.) • Vietnam

When asked to offer advice about success, I am reminded of the advice my high school football coach, Clancy Smith, a wounded WWI veteran, gave me. After the final game of a one-and-seven losing season, I said, "I'm sorry, Coach, I guess we're just a bunch of losers." I still remember his words, "Son, whether you think this team is a bunch of losers or a bunch of winners, you're right."

The next day I told Coach Smith, "I don't understand, what do you mean by 'whether you think you're a loser or a winner, you're right'?" He explained, "The difference between success and failure is you, and it's a choice."

I am an ex-Navy fighter pilot with 75 combat missions over Vietnam. If I had it all to do over again, I would stop at seventy-four. The Vietnamese cell I was in was eight feet long and eight feet wide. I could only pace three steps one way, then turn around and pace three steps the other. Inside this cell, there were no books to read, no window to look out, no TV, telephone, or radio. I didn't have a pencil or a piece of paper for 2,103 days.

I spent six years at the "University of Hanoi," and I received a degree in hard knocks. It was a long time to pace three steps in one direction and then three steps in the other. I would not wish it on anyone. I would, however, tell you it was the most valuable six years of my life.

For two of the almost six years I was a POW in Vietnam, I served as the chaplain to the POWs. I feel I must stress the importance of faith as a key to significance. Finally, if there is one single thing I validated in that Communist prison camp, it's this: Coach Smith was right! The difference between failure, success and also significance is you, and it's your choice!

FORGIVING THE UNFORGIVABLE

I was really angry...angry at my government for sending me to Vietnam, angry at myself for getting shot down, and angry at my God for not sending a miracle to rescue my co-pilot and me when our F-4 Phantom was shot out of the sky. And perhaps most of all, I was angry at the enemy for the torture and brutality—the sheer physical pain they had brought to my body for no apparent reason. I lay on the prison floor and bled and wept.

I had no idea at that moment in time the significance of my experience and the impact it would have on the rest of my life. In fact, I was convinced that the most value this time could ever have would be a period of my life I could someday forget! It would take months of anguish to teach me a vital lesson. And even today, having had many years to reflect on the experience, I'm still learning and growing from being a prisoner of war for six years in North Vietnam.

In some ways, my psychological response seemed to follow the Kubler-Ross model in her book, *Death and Dying*. I can track her five stages pretty clearly in my experience. I was first in denial, having flown that supersonic jet through the sky thinking I was bullet proof. I couldn't believe anyone in the world had a gun big enough to shoot down Charlie Plumb. (The pain of the first bayonet stab in my thigh quickly brought me out of that fantasy and into the next stage.)

Kubler-Ross's second stage, anger, is where I dwelt the longest and learned the most. (Remember it took me years to finally understand and appreciate all this.) At that time I really wanted to kill something or someone. And I felt totally justified in that feeling. After all, by any intelligent analysis, I was the quintessential victim of circumstances beyond my control; I was 24 years old with a new wife back home, a graduate of the Naval Academy with a great future ahead of us. Why me, Lord?

But my formula for the most indelible lesson of life is this: L=PT. In order to Learn something, it takes a certain amount of Pain times a certain amount of Time. And for me this lesson took a considerable amount of pain for about three months. That's how long it took for me to move on to the next stage. Kubler-Ross calls it acceptance. I chose to think of it as forgiveness.

An engineer by education, I tried to reason this through. First I started to consider the consequences of anger. It became pretty clear to me that no matter how much rage I could muster, I wasn't going to affect the outcome of the war (which had been, as a military guy, my primary mission). In fact my wrath seemed to actually encourage my enemy. And in harboring all this vitriol, I was eating myself up from the inside out! Assuming I still had the choice, it just didn't seem very profitable to harbor any negative feelings.

So I found a new definition for anger. Using our secret communication system, a fellow POW gave me this anonymous definition: "Anger: an acid which does more harm to the vessel in which it is stored than to the subject onto which it is poured." When I heard that, I was sure that I was that vessel. But even understanding that, the next questions were the biggest. If I can't pour the acid on something, how on earth do I get rid of it? How do I change my attitude? How do I ignore the atrocities perpetrated on me and my pals? After much searching, I found it to be a simple tool, sometimes easy to say but difficult to implement: unconditional forgiveness. It worked in the prison, and it works today.

I had been a Christian since the age of 13, but I didn't have a clue to the meaning of Christ's purpose on earth until my six years as a POW. Different from any religion I have studied, Christianity is based on unconditional forgiveness. That's what God's grace is to me. And that's what Christ requests of each of us.

And it isn't just forgiving our enemies, sometimes it's forgiving ourselves. This, in turn, gives us permission to step forward and move on with our lives. I'm convinced that we can imprison ourselves with guilt and self-doubt so that we become paralyzed. And those mental prison walls can be more restrictive than the ones of stone and steel I was behind in the prison camps in Vietnam. We set ourselves free when we forgive.

So the act of forgiveness can be a selfish one. (I think it's okay to be selfish once in a while.) Because if you can keep a forgiving heart, you can keep a healthy heart. So forgive the unforgivable...for the good of others, for yourself, and for your God.

Murray Pritchard
WWII • ETO

I was blessed to serve as a medic in WWII. I returned home and continued my education and obtained advanced degrees in science and medicine. I would like to encourage every young man and woman to continue their education. Education is extremely important, and it allows one many opportunities in life. Hard work is also a part of the process of finding success in life. To find significance in life, you must have faith in God, trust in Him, and make a commitment to Him. Remember also to treat others the way you want to be treated and live by the Golden Rule everyday!

PROVIDENCE

I was a Corporal in the 109th Medical Battalion of the 34th Division during World War II. I was one of five corpsmen attached to the 168th Infantry along with a physician and an ambulance driver. The 168th was ordered to defend Faid Pass in Tunisia. On February 14, 1943, forces under the command of General Rommel broke through the pass and surrounded our unit. With only one company of infantrymen and only a few tanks, the decision was made to withdraw to a plateau known as Garet Hadid. Even with the withdrawal, we were still totally surrounded in a sea of German troops.

We were under constant bombardment from German tanks, 88-mm guns, and sniper fire. The wounded and the dying were brought to our small temporary first-aid station where we attempted to give them the best care we could under the circumstances. We were unable to evacuate the wounded to a field hospital because we could not get through the German lines. The facilities at the aid station were so bad that we did an intestinal surgical repair one night, using a flashlight so the physician could see. We used our ambulance as an operating room. Later the same night, it was riddled with gunfire. I was working with the wounded continuously and had no time to sleep. It was my duty to dress the wounds, give medication, check for abnormal or excessive bleeding, and to help feed those who could eat.

Early on the morning of February 15th, I began my medical rounds. I had five patients lying on litters placed end to end in a ravine. I had just checked two of the patients when I stood and began to walk up the ravine. To my right, I saw dirt, rocks, and debris falling along the slope of the ravine. Initially I paid little attention to it, believing it must be an animal scurrying away. Checking another patient, I stood and once again noticed dirt, rocks, and debris falling along the right side of the ravine. This caught my attention, and I continued my duties with greater caution. This happened a third time. Wearily I bent down to check the next patient as bullets passed right beside my head. Apparently when I was standing, I could be seen by a sniper but I was safe in a crouched position. As I surveyed the rock rim along the mountain, I could see the shadow of a German soldier waiting to kill any unsuspecting GI.

I headed back down the ravine in a stooped position and reported the incident to two young infantrymen. After I identified the area where the sniper was hiding, they took off and circled behind him. About an hour later, we heard gunfire and the young soldiers both yelled, "We got him."

Some might believe that the falling dirt, rock, and debris was a coincidence. Not me! I am convinced that this was a providential incident that God used to get my attention and to spare my life...in order for me to care for other wounded soldiers.

Chief Warrant Officer Charles Pruitt
U.S. Navy (Ret.) • WWII • PTO

My creed or motto for life is: Don't become dependent on others, but know when to ask for help and be willing to accept it when it is offered.

HELP ONE ANOTHER

I was a veteran of the Philippine campaign in the early days of WWII, having served on both the Bataan Peninsula and the island fortress of Corregidor. I spent 41 months as a prisoner of war of the Japanese, surviving both the slave labor camps in the Philippines and Japan, and the "Hellships" transporting the POWs to Japan and other foreign lands. I would credit my survival to my faith in God, country, self, and my comrades. We helped one another when help was needed without becoming dependent on each other. When help was needed in the form of moral support, it was always there without the asking.

Colonel Benjamin Purcell
U.S. Army (Ret.) • Vietnam

Life is God's gift to you. A life well lived is your gift to God. Every moment is precious and should not be wasted for there is no guarantee of tomorrow. So live, that when you die, your Lord will say, "Well done, good and faithful servant" (Matthew 25:23).

LIGHT TO MY PATH

In early April 1968, my POW group, which had been captured in South Vietnam in February, was being moved to North Vietnam along the Ho Chi Minh Trail. We traveled at night to avoid detection. By then my legs were covered with infected sores from untreated leech bites. Malnutrition, forced marches, diarrhea, and infections were taking a heavy toll on me. I could manage fine when I was sitting, but standing and walking were sheer agony. When I was on the ground resting, I was never sure whether I would be able to get up again.

One night was exceptionally dark, and I couldn't see to walk. For several minutes I stumbled along, tripping on unseen roots and rocks. Each ditch and rut in the road became a major obstacle. I felt tired, beaten, and almost helpless. I knew if I fell and couldn't get up, I was going to be shot because the head man had already given that order. I was no longer the confident, self-sufficient, infantry officer I had been two months earlier. I needed help. I needed a light, and that's exactly what I asked for in the simple prayer of a desperate man.

"Lord, I've got to have a light here, because I cannot see to walk, and I'm not going to survive this march unless I can keep up with the others."

I will always believe that what happened next was a miracle. Within a minute, the guide, who until now had been content to walk in darkness, turned on a flashlight and directed the beam right at my feet. He kept it there for the remainder of the night. Never before had God answered my prayer so dramatically and so soon.

"If you believe, you will receive whatever you ask for in prayer" (Matthew 21:22).

Dudley Riley
WWII • ETO

My code of conduct for life has been to establish a firm foundation in God and family and serve them in the ways in which I have been called upon to do so. My advice for life is to make every effort to help those who cannot help themselves.

I SING BECAUSE I'M FREE

As a young boy growing up in rural Kentucky and the youngest of nine children, the value of the family unit was strongly emphasized. Because of my strong family foundations and my Christian upbringing, the desire to live and to be of service to others was firmly established in me prior to my years spent as a POW in World War II.

Today I am grateful that I have been given the opportunities to serve and to help others through my involvement with the Red Cross Disaster Relief, teaching Sunday school to the elderly that are homebound, lecturing elementary and high school students about my experiences as a prisoner of war, and working with exchange students to help with the English language and history of the United States.

I retired from the Veterans Administration after 35 years. I was elected to serve as State Commander of the Kentucky Department of Ex-Prisoners of War in 1996-1997 and again in 1998-1999. I have been commander of the local western Kentucky Chapter since its formation in February 1995. I am proud to work with my fellow Ex-POW friends to make life better for all Americans. After all, "We exist to help those who cannot help themselves." This brings to mind the words of the grand old hymn:

> I sing because I'm happy
> I sing because I'm free.
> His eye is on the sparrow
> And I know He watches me.

Norman Rippee
WWII • ETO

My advice for life is serve God, nation and others! Just as we are told to love God and to love our neighbors, there is no greater success and no greater significance than to serve.

IN THE HANDS OF GOD

I was inducted into the Army Air Corps in 1942. I volunteered for gunnery school, becoming a flight engineer on a combat crew of a B-26 Bomber of the 319th Bombardment Group. After graduation we were sent to North Africa. We had ten crews in our class, two of which crashed with no survivors. This was perhaps the first of many times in my life when I knew our lives were in the hand of God.

From North Africa we went to Sardinia and then Corsica. On October 19, 1944, I was on my 22nd mission in the Po Valley of Italy when I was shot down by Luftwaffe ME109 fighter planes. We all parachuted out and immediately became prisoners of war. Again, I knew His hand would protect me.

I was picked up by soldiers of the Africa Korps and sent to northwest Poland, to the prison camp of Stalag Luft IV. On February 6, 1944, the Luftwaffe marched us out of Luft IV because the Russian Army would soon overrun the camp. We marched west, sleeping in barns and sometimes outside on the ground for 86 days. During this period we never removed our clothing or our shoes. Food and water were scarce. I lost a great deal of weight.

On May 2, 1945, the English 2nd Army caught up with us approximately 100 kilometers east of Hamburg, Germany. We had covered approximately 600 miles on this forced march. We arrived at the Canadian base in Brussels on May 8, 1945. I never once doubted that I would return home.

I feel fortunate to be a citizen of this country. Even though I came out of WWII with some physical and mental scars, they have healed long ago. If called upon to do it again, I would gladly go. God bless America!

Brigadier General Robinson Risner
U.S. Air Force (Ret.) • Vietnam

Few people have reached their goals without determination. During my 33-year Air Force career, I was surrounded by people who were better educated, had a higher IQ, and many with greater talent. However, few had more determination. In addition, I had a strong faith in God. Determination and faith in God are the lynch pins that will take you to your goal.

YOU PASSED

When I was a child, my older brother learned how to fly small airplanes and that became my dream. World War II started when I was in high school, and I dreamed of becoming a fighter pilot. During high school I decided to attend Bible College, but I still wanted to be a pilot. I was only 17 when I graduated from high school and really wanted to enter the Aviation Cadet Program. One of the requirements to be accepted into the program was that you had to be a college graduate. I realized that I didn't have a chance, but one day while reading the paper, I read an article that said if you could pass a two-year college entrance exam, then you could apply to become an aviation cadet. I was only a mediocre student, but I immediately began to pray about the opportunity. Previously I had decided that I was going to go to Bible College, but I prayed, "Lord, if it is okay for me to go into the military...help me pass that test."

I was accepted to take the four hour examination. I was the last one to complete it. Everyone else had already finished and left. I handed my test to the sergeant who administered the test and started to leave. He said, "Wait a minute. We're not supposed to give out scores, but in your case, I'm going to make an exception." He graded the test, looked up at me, and said, "You passed by one point." I knew the Lord was saying, "It's OK."

In Vietnam I came to the conclusion that nothing was more important than a faith in God. Before imprisonment many of us had been too busy to put God first in our lives. A North Vietnamese prison cell changed that. We learned to feel at ease in talking about God, and we shared our doubts and faith. We prayed for one another and spent time praying together for all kinds of things. Our faith in God was essential. Without it, I could not have survived.

Master Sergeant Arlo Robb
U.S. Army (Ret.) • Korea

While in the military and also in civilian life afterward, I've always tried to be a good leader and set the example for those under me. I always tried to be fair and strict. I was both surprised and gratified to hear from a former subordinate after 47 years. We had served together in Europe in the late 50s and early 60s. I didn't remember him initially, but he certainly remembered me. I had to look him up in an old picture reference to refresh my memory. He told me that at the time he wanted to be transferred to my unit, which had scored near the top in many Army Training Tests (graded tactical operations). I was the platoon leader, as we rarely had a lieutenant assigned. I was pleased to learn that he subsequently went to Officer Candidate School, and in his long career as an officer, applied my fair but strict principles. I can only hope that the example he said I displayed had an impact on the soldiers beyond my career.

As a prisoner of war, the combination of severe deprivation and near-death injuries engendered in me a close bond with my fellow prisoners that simply cannot be duplicated in civilian life. In particular, the care of my British fellow prisoners delivered me from certain death and helped me appreciate the value of God's gift of life, and the power of hope and the human spirit in very difficult conditions.

THERE ARE NO ATHEISTS IN FOXHOLES— GOD HAD A PLAN

It's said that there are no atheists in a war-time foxhole. My foxhole was a ditch along a road just north of Hoengsong in what would later be called "Massacre Valley." I was not a Christian at the outset of the Korean conflict and had little to live for. In fact, I extended my enlistment one year to go to Korea. Under orders from President Truman, I deployed with Company K, 338th Infantry Regiment, of the 2nd Infantry Division from Fort Lewis, Washington. We arrived and helped save the entire Korean Peninsula from being overrun by Communist North Korean forces.

When the Chinese entered the fight in November 1950, K Company was surrounded and essentially destroyed. On November 27, 1950, during a fighting withdrawal on the road south to Kunu, I was struck by four bullets and wounded. Fortunately for me, only one hit its mark squarely in my leg; the others were just grazing wounds. During my evacuation, the ambulance was stopped and inspected by Chinese soldiers. I guess they did not want to contend with wounded prisoners because they directed us to continue on to our forces.

The Army doctors managed to save my badly injured leg. They declared me fit for duty, and I returned to Company K in early February 1951. It was cold but clear on February 11 as we accompanied a convoy of artillery and tanks on the main road between Hoengsong and Saemai. As we marched through the valley, we came under fire from the Chinese Forces. Within minutes Chinese forces had destroyed the lead and the rear vehicles, trapping the convoy in a classic ambush. On the left, the Chinese had complete control of the heights overlooking our column. On our right was a marsh that was impassible to our vehicles. We returned fire, and the fighting continued throughout the day and into the night. As night passed into morning, it became apparent that we were completely surrounded and that there was no chance of re-supply or reinforcement. We recovered ammunition from burning vehicles, and fought wave after wave of Chinese soldiers, literally killing hundreds at point-blank range. At one point, lying flat on the road, another soldier and I fired a .30 caliber water-cooled machine gun without the benefit of a tripod to hold off each wave. One of us held the base of the machine gun while the other pivoted the machine gun to direct the fire to where the threat was greatest.

By early morning on February 12, we were down to nine soldiers and were running critically low on ammunition. The remaining officer in command of our dwindling forces decided that we could not continue to defend ourselves, and that there was no possibility of linking up with our forces to the south. With that decision I began my time as a prisoner of war, spending just under three years in "Bean Camp" and camps 1 and 4. While I was a POW, I experienced scabies, almost died of dysentery, and nearly lost my leg. If it weren't for the British soldiers confined with us, I would not have survived my captivity. They bandaged my leg in salt and nursed me back to health, even though my captors had considered me a hopeless case and had placed me in the "Death House."

After the armistice, I was released to Allied forces at Panmunjon. I'll never forget a brigadier general there who helped me dismount from the back of the truck. I weighed less than 130 lbs and was elated to be free. Clearly I was blessed to survive my wounds and my POW incarceration, and I am deeply thankful. I was convinced that God had a plan for me, even when I was in that foxhole. Because of my experience, I grew spiritually, and I was able to maintain a unique perspective about life. Experiencing the horror of war is one of the worst things a person can endure. The difficult and even terrible experience enabled me to confront routine problems and difficulties with greater confidence. The experience also increased my trust in God, and helped me accept that things do and will work out for the best.

THE STAR SPANGLED BANNER

Oh, say can you see by the dawn's early light

What so proudly we hailed at the twilight's last gleaming?

Whose broad stripes and bright stars thru the perilous fight,

O'er the ramparts we watched were so gallantly streaming?

And the rocket's red glare, the bombs bursting in air,

Gave proof through the night that our flag was still there.

Oh, say does that star spangled banner yet wave

O'er the land of the free and the home of the brave?

Zach Roberts
WWII • ETO
Past National Commander
American Ex-POW Association 1999-2000

In Proverbs 20:7 we read, "The man of integrity, his children will be blessed after him." It is my conviction that the most significant legacy we can provide our children and grandchildren is a strong sense of religious and moral values.

TESTED

My maternal grandmother taught herself to read and write, and taught adult Bible classes; from her I learned faith, honesty, and integrity. My maternal grandfather was a coal miner who suffered multiple severe injuries; from him I learned strength in adversity. At the height of the depression years, my mother opened a successful business; from her I learned the value of hard work. From my father I learned to have kindness and compassion for the less fortunate, and a positive attitude.

I make slide presentations to every new class at the Non-Commissioned Officer Academy at McGuire Air Force Base, and their most commonly asked question is how I endured 15 months of captivity and post-traumatic stress. My response is that in every person's life they will face a time of crisis, with no one to turn to. Alcohol and drugs cannot solve our problems. I am not a preacher, but I am a believer. I credit faith, the belief that it is the grace of God that gives us the support and guidance to persevere. I am alive today because of Him. It has been the legacy of this faith that told me God watched over me, and Jesus walked with me.

My faith was tested today. As I was writing this advice I was informed my son, Master Sergeant Zach Sheldon Roberts, age 47, had died of a massive heart attack. I am comforted knowing that God will watch over him, and Jesus will walk with him.

Ralph Rodriguez, Jr.
WWII • PTO
Past National Commander
American Ex-POW Association 1964-1965

My advice to the young and the old is this: When you help those in need, you're doing God's work. When you're dedicated to God's work, you will overcome any difficulties.

—◆•◆•◆—

THANK GOD, I AM A SURVIVOR

More than a half century ago, I was drafted into the service of my country. As a young man, I had never been away from home, but I was more prepared than I realized. I knew that my tour of duty was for one year, and I was proud of being a soldier. As soldiers we didn't walk to town, we marched in cadence. Within a few months we overcame the recruit status; we were real soldiers. Suddenly everything I was taught at home by my parents started to come into play. Being one of ten brothers and sisters, I knew how to obey authority. Being true and honest to my superiors was not my first test. I was educated in Catholic school, by nuns, and grew up in a community that practiced faith, honesty, integrity, and good moral values; they were embedded in our minds.

After about six months, our regiment was on its way to the Philippines. The possibility of war expressed by our leaders maintained that we were a great and powerful nation, and if Japan dared to attack us, we would destroy them within six months. How wrong we were!

On December 8, 1941, at 7 a.m., just as we stepped out of church, we heard that the Japanese had bombed Pearl Harbor. The damage was reported as being enormous, and the loss of life was great. At 12:25 p.m., just after lunch, the beginning of what we thought would be a six-month war started. The first 30 minutes after the Japanese bombers dropped their bombs on Clark Field, I was headed for the hospital. I was a medic, but a soldier called me to help him feed ammunition to his 50 caliber machine gun. We emptied four boxes of ammunition at the dive bombers. The planes strafed us, but we kept firing. About 5 p.m., I was on my way to Nichols Field in the city of Manila. The enemy continued to bomb us constantly.

By the end of December we were sent to the Bataan peninsula. Our resistance began to crumble against a powerful enemy with a great number of troops. This was the beginning of the end of the predicted six month war. There was complete cooperation in an attempt to survive. We all helped each other. As our numbers decreased, we gained strength and determination against the enemy. I searched my soul to find answers about our future.

Our Catholic priest came once a week to hold chapel services. I asked the chaplain his honest opinion of what was in store for us. His answer was a shock to my ears when he said, "Surrender!" It's difficult to explain the emotional preparation for surrender. The commander of the medical company, holding a white flag, walked down the hill towards the road where enemy tanks were waiting. We faced the enemy, their machine guns pointed directly at us. Our six month war came to an end in four brutal months. We were suffering from disease and hunger. We were out of ammunition, food, and medical supplies.

Once again the character I had developed from my childhood and as a young man, suddenly began to spring into action—love thy neighbor, feed the hungry, care for the sick. As a medic, that was my duty until the last day of imprisonment.

On January 30, 1945, at 7:30 p.m., the 6th Ranger Battalion rescued about 511 weak, sick men. Once again we marched, but this time we marched the freedom march. We marched all night, and by noon the next day we reached the American lines.

John Romine
WWII • ETO
National Chaplain
American Ex-POW Association

In Luke 6:31, we read, "Do unto others as you would have them do unto you." It important to live by the Golden Rule. Make a conscious effort to treat others the way you would like to be treated.

A CUP OF WATER

As a child during the depression days in Oklahoma, so many things seemed huge and awesome and far too great for my understanding—the great prayers and sermons at church, the sheriff, and leaders of our community. Then I was caught up in a World War. I flew 43 combat missions of the most hellish kind in a B-24 bomber. I was shot down over Northern Italy and became a POW in Germany for 11 months of hunger, thirst, sickness, fear, cold, and filth.

After liberation and returning home, I was in total shock and refused to participate in worship, church services, or honoring a God who would allow people to go through what happened to me.

Then one day I read Matthew 25. I remembered what a few swallows of water had meant to me. Late one night we were on a forced march from one POW camp to another. As we passed through a small village, a total stranger reached through an open window and handed me a cup of water. I had found the healing of my pain in the memory of that cup of water, and I went to work for the Lord, lending a helping hand when and where I could. Even small deeds are eternal.

Chief Warrant Officer Wilburn Rowden
ARNG (Ret.) • WWII • ETO

You need courage to accomplish your assigned goals even under the most adverse conditions. I observed this evidence of courage during my confinement, harassment, and harsh conditions as a POW. When the future looked bleak, those men with courage made the best of the situation. This also included careful planning to eliminate or circumvent the obstacles that could hinder or prevent accomplishment of their assigned or personal goals.

Faith plays a great part in accomplishing your goals. My observation is that faith is greatest under the most adverse conditions. As a POW I observed young men eager to learn more of the Bible and its teachings. Of the few classes that were permitted, those about the Bible were attended by more young soldiers than any other. We were allowed to have church services on occasion, and the attendance attested to a faith and a belief in God.

You need consideration for people you are working with and especially the people you are training or leading. A sense of caring for their safety and well-being will make them respectful of you as their teacher and leader. Work to gain the respect of people with whom you work and associate.

You need a love of country. The POW was always expressing and displaying a love of country. They were looking forward to the day they would return to the United States and our way of life.

PROUD TO BE AN AMERICAN

I was born in Maries County, Missouri, on a small farm. I was the first of six children. Originally, we did not have electricity or indoor plumbing in our home. We lived in rather primitive conditions according to today's standards. We used kerosene lamps for light at night and a wash tub in which to bathe. Dad used a battery-operated radio to get the local news, and we were able to listen to the Grand Ole Opry in Nashville on Saturday nights. We used horses to pull farm equipment to till the fields. On Sundays we went to church in the farm wagon pulled by a team of horses. It was a Sunday ritual that we rarely missed. I remember one of my assignments in Sunday school class was to memorize the names of the books of the New Testament and recite them before the class.

I attended a rural, one-room school during my primary school years. All eight grades were taught by one teacher. I walked the one-half mile to school and carried my lunch in a used, tin lard container. We all sat at wooden desks and shared the drinking water from a bucket using the same dipper. The water was drawn from a well with a bucket. My first year in high school I walked about three miles each day to catch a school bus to ride 14 miles to the high school. I graduated in 1941. We continued to attend church as a family every Sunday, but by that time we used a Ford automobile for transportation.

Being a backwoods country boy with a high school diploma and no experience in anything except farming, I found my introduction to the military in 1943 as a new adventure. One of my first stations was Miami, Florida, and we were billeted in a hotel. It was quite a change from the country style living I was accustomed to, and I considered myself lucky to be in the Army Air Corps. I was trained as a radio operator and as a crew member of a B-17 Bomber aircraft. Our 10-man crew came from nine different states. We became a close-knit crew, sharing and caring for each other. On Christmas Eve 1943, we boarded a troop train headed for our port of embarkation. On New Year's Eve we boarded the British ship, the "Queen Elizabeth" and sailed for England. The air base that we were assigned to was being built when we arrived. The enlisted men were assigned quarters in Quonset huts, and we all shared the job of preparing our aircraft for the missions ahead.

On March 8, 1944, we drew a target in Berlin, Germany. On our way to the target near Hannover, Germany, we were attacked and hit by German fighter aircraft. We lost our number 2 engine and sustained other damage to the aircraft that forced us to fall out of formation. When that happened, we were repeatedly attacked and sustained major damage to our aircraft. The nose, radio room, and the tail of the plane were all damaged, and we also lost hydraulics. Over the intercom the pilot gave the order to the crew to prepare to bail out. The navigator replied to the pilot saying, "Mack, the 20-mm shell that hit the nose of the plane destroyed my parachute and the parachute of the bombardier...we don't have any parachutes." The pilot immediately responded, giving the order to stand by and to disregard the order to bail out. Each crew member responded except the tail gunner. There was pandemonium in the plane. The navigator, tail gunner, and the radio operator (myself) were all wounded. I could hear the discussion between the co-pilot and pilot saying that we couldn't continue to a suitable landing area. Once again, the pilot came on the intercom and summoned the navigator to the nose of the aircraft. He ordered the navigator to take the pilot's parachute and the bombardier to take the only spare parachute remaining, and for the crew to bail out. The navigator protested, but the pilot commanded the crew to obey the order.

As we prepared to bail out of the crippled aircraft, the tail gunner had crawled forward to the waist position of the plane and was lying on the floor. He had been wounded in the hand. The two waist gunners hooked a static line to his parachute and pushed him out of the plane. As I started to head to the waist position to bail out, I realized that the ball turret was jammed and the gunner could not get out. With the help of the flight engineer, we manually cranked the turret to a position where the gunner was able to get out. We then exited the plane, leaving the pilot to attempt to crash-land. The pilot was able to do so and survived. Two of the crew, the co-pilot and the bombardier, were apparently killed by ground fire. The remaining crew was captured.

As a POW in Germany, I witnessed many acts of kindness that made me respect my comrades. We endured many harsh experiences. In July of 1944, we were held in the hold of coal barges traveling from Stalag Luft VI in Poland to Germany. We were met by German soldiers with fixed bayonets and guard dogs, handcuffed, and then forced to move double-time from the train depot to Stalag Luft IV. In the winter of 1945, from February to April we endured a 500-mile march. Without the help of fellow POWs, many of us would not have made it. We shared everything, including food, so others might survive.

As a prisoner of war, I saw acts of kindness and compassion over and over by POWs. I believe this experience helped to make me a better person. At times I also witnessed acts by some of our German guards that made me realize there is some good in almost all people. During my experience as a POW, I came to the conclusion that there was Someone who was watching over us and caring for us. One of my most vivid memories is of the town of Nance, France. I saw a church with a tall steeple that remained untouched while buildings all around had been destroyed. This instance reminds me even today that when everything around us seems to be falling apart, the one thing we still have is our faith.

As I look back at my time as a POW, I realize that I am a better person because of the experience. As a young country boy, I saw and learned much. I am able to say that I am proud to be an American and to have had the opportunity to serve my country!

Clifford Savage
WWII • Germany

I don't feel like I am qualified to give expert advice to anyone, but my advice for life is: Always be willing to help your fellow man and never try to impose your will on someone else. I believe that having a faith in God is the most important thing a person can accomplish. With God, everything is possible. I know that without God, my life would be empty. He is my friend, my Lord, and my Savior.

I PRAYED OFTEN AND EARNESTLY

I was born in Lafayette country, near Oxford, Mississippi, on December 30, 1919. I was the fourth of five children. My mother died when I was only two years old, and we moved to the community of Orwood when I was about three years old. We lived on a farm that was known as the Cook place, and raised cotton, corn, and soybeans. During the Depression, we did not have much but were happy, and I was young enough that I didn't know any better. In 1939 I joined the Civilian Conservation Corps for two years. I moved to Memphis and got a job working in a mop factory with a starting wage of $18 a week. At the time, that was big money to me.

In November 1942, I was drafted into the Army and began my time in the service at Fort Oglethorpe, Georgia. From Fort Oglethorpe, I went to Camp Van Dorn and was assigned to the 99th Infantry Division. I received additional training in Louisiana and Texas.

In 1944 we headed for Europe, first to England, then France, and finally Belgium where we entered combat in November. On December 6th, with the beginning of the Battle of the Bulge, we were surrounded by the enemy and forced to surrender. Initially we were forced to carry the German dead and wounded back to their bunkers. Late at night we were put on a train and traveled in boxcars for four days without food or water. I was a POW in Moosburg for a short period time but was moved to a work detail. While assigned to this work detail and with the advance of allied troops, American troops overtook us on April 29, 1945.

Looking back on the events of my life, I know that I have been blessed more than I deserve. God has blessed me with a wonderful family. In June 2001, I lost my wife of 52 years. I am proud to say that I am a true believer in Jesus Christ. I was saved in 1958, but I admit that I always knew there was a God. As a POW I prayed often and earnestly to Him. I continue to pray every day for greater faith and for our nation. The most important thought I would give to the young people of America is to always have faith in God and be willing if necessary to give your life for your country. There is no greater country than the USA!

Major Allen Seamans
U.S. Air Force (Ret.) • WWII • ETO

My advice for life is: Never give up! It would have been easy to give up on one of the long, cold days in Stalag Luft III. We had very little to do, even less to eat, and we didn't know if we would ever be liberated. It is profoundly important to always have hope! I would also encourage everyone to live by the Golden Rule...treat others the way you want to be treated.

FREE AT LAST

I spent one year and one month in Europe during World War II. I received a lot of help, both physical and emotional. The first three months I was cared for by the Dutch underground. I depended on them for food, clothing, shelter, and protection from the Germans. During the last ten months, I depended on an even greater authority—I depended on God!

I was captured by the Germans and was initially held in Stalag Luft III at Sagan, Germany. We were fortunate and blessed to have a very conscientious Chaplain named Brother Daniels. He held religious services twice on Sunday and also on special occasions during the week. I made it a point to never miss one of these services, and I ended every single night in prayer. I believe everyone did the same. Those services and those prayers helped to get us through a very difficult time.

Over the course of three months, three things happened. First, we were moved out of Stalag III. The snow on the ground was about 18" deep. We had to carry everything we owned. Second, we were forced to walk for five days, sleeping in the open with almost no shelter. Third, the Germans had very little food so we received a limited amount to eat.

At the end of this march, we were loaded into boxcars. We spent five more days in rail travel to Moosberg in southern Germany, about 30 miles north of Munich. We spent the rest of the war in Stalag VIIA. We were fortunate because everyone that I knew in my group survived, but we all lost a significant amount of weight. Stalag VII was a miserable place in every aspect, including the food, the weather, and general living conditions.

On Sunday, April 29, 1945, we watched as the Stars and Stripes was raised in Moosberg by soldiers of General Patton's 14th Armored Division. Brother Daniels held the last and, I guess, most important service of all. We thanked God for His mercy and grace and that we were free at last!

Roy Shenkel
WWII • ETO

My advice for life is: Read your Testament! These words were spoken to me during World War II when I was a prisoner of war. The words had a tremendous impact on my life, and the statement has directed my steps for 60 years. The Scriptural reference is Psalm 119:105, "Your word is a lamp to my feet and a light for my path."

LORD, I'M YOURS IF YOU WANT ME

I enlisted in the Army Air Corp, in October 1942 when I was 19 years old. I spent my 20th birthday as a prisoner of war. Initially I trained as an aircraft mechanic and gunner and was assigned as a right waist gunner on a B-17 Bomber to the 463rd Bomb Group, the 774th Bomb Squadron. On my fourth mission, on April 6, 1944, we were to bomb the marshaling yards at Zagreb, Yugoslavia. Approaching the target we were attacked by fighters and hit by a rocket in the bomb bay of the of the B-17. There was a huge explosion, and the plane immediately burst into flames. At the time we were flying at 25,000 feet, so I bailed out of the aircraft at an altitude of over 20,000 feet. Due to the lack of oxygen, I passed out, regaining consciousness just in time to deploy my parachute. I hit the ground so hard that I broke my ankle. When I was captured, I was interrogated and sent to a hospital in Graz, Austria for two months. I eventually spent time as a prisoner of war in Stalag Luft IV in Poland and Stalag Luft I in Barth, Germany.

I was a POW for 13 months and one week. The winter of 1944 was the coldest winter on record. In the morning we had to stand outside for roll call in snow that was up to our knees. We only had a small amount of coal to burn to heat our building. The barracks were built on stilts so no one could make an escape by using a tunnel. The fact that the buildings were off the ground made them even colder. We were always cold and hungry. The Germans never gave us our full parcel from the Red Cross so our food was usually potatoes, black bread, which contained sawdust, and coffee made from acorns.

To keep the POWs from being liberated, many were force marched across Germany. I guess I was blessed to have fractured my ankle because it saved me from being in the death march. However, I did spend seven days and eight nights in a boxcar with 50 other prisoners when I was moved to Stalag Luft I. During the move, we received no food and very little water; it was so cold that my hair froze solid.

I was not a Christian when I entered the service. In fact, I now know that had I been killed in that burning B-17, I would have spent an eternity in hell. While I was a prisoner I received a small Gideon New Testament in a Red Cross package. I still remember the words of a prisoner who I had never seen before and never saw again. He said, "Roy, read your Testament!" To this day I wonder if it might have been the words of an angel.

After I started to read the small Bible, the stories and the words took on a new meaning, and I found hope and faith. I still remember to this day the exact spot and the time of day when I walked up to the barracks, looked up toward heaven, and said, "Lord, I'm yours if you want me."

Rear Admiral Robert Shumaker
U.S. Navy (Ret.) • Vietnam

Paradoxically, I learned a lot about life from my experience as a prisoner of war in Vietnam. Those tough lessons learned within a jail cell have application to all those who will never have to undergo that particular trauma. At some point in life, everybody will be hungry, cold, lonely, extorted, sick, humiliated, or fearful, in varying degrees of intensity. It is the manner in which you react to these challenges that will distinguish you.

When adversity strikes, you need to fall back with the punch and do your best to get up off the mat to come back for the next round. A person is not in total control of his destiny, but you need to know what your goals are, and you have to prepare yourself in advance to take advantage of opportunity when that door opens. Some important tools on the road to success include the ability and willingness to communicate, treating those around you with respect and courtesy no matter what their station in life might be, and conducting your life with the morality and behavior that will allow you to face yourself...for in the end, you alone must be your own harshest critic.

THE IMPORTANCE OF HUMOR

You can sometimes find humor in the most bizarre circumstances, and that humorous moment can often sustain your spirits in spite of the unpleasant surroundings. Such was the case one time during my Vietnamese imprisonment. The food was meager and monotonous, and after nearly three years of solitary confinement, I could barley stand up without experiencing dizziness. The yearly diet consisted of three months of pumpkin soup, three months of sewer greens, and six long months of cabbage soup. You can imagine how weary one becomes after six months of cabbage soup. We were forbidden to talk to each other or make any sound and so, quite unexpectedly, during one of the noisy bombardments by American jet fighters and equally noisy Anti-Aircraft gunfire, I heard a distinctive American voice shouting. He was directing his message to the pilots (as if they could hear him). "Bomb the cabbage patches!" was his directive, and it brought down the house in laughter.

NINE FEET TALL

Two years before our release, the Vietnamese moved us into a central location and let us live together in groups of 75 or so men. Having endured solitary confinement, we were elated to be with other Americans. Nevertheless one Sunday, when we tried to hold a quiet church service in our cell block, the Vietnamese suspected us of sinister plotting and stormed the compound with fixed bayonets. As they marched off three "ringleaders," the remaining guys started singing "The Star Spangled Banner" with near-deafening volume. After six weeks of solitary confinement, the stalwart threesome returned. We asked one of them how it felt to hear the national anthem after nearly five years of imposed silence. Colonel Risner said, "I felt as if I could go bear hunting with a switch; in fact, I felt nine feet tall!" Years later, after our release, Mr. Ross Perot commissioned a sculptor to cast a bronze statue of Colonel Risner. It stands on the campus of the U.S. Air Force Academy as a reminder to cadets about what true courage really means. The statue is exactly nine feet tall.

HELPING OTHERS

Two years into our imprisonment, the Vietnamese were bearing down on us to make anti-war propaganda. One technique was to withhold food and water until the POW was compliant. At the time we were held in the old French movie colony we called the Zoo. We lived in somewhat large rooms in solitary confinement or sometimes with a cellmate. Through our tap code communication method, we knew that one of our group was getting the starvation treatment. A week without food or water makes a man really weak. One of our guys waited for the siesta hour and managed (only God knows how) to climb up to the ceiling which must have been 15 feet high. He opened a hatch, climbed into the attic, moved over to where the tortured POW's cell was located, and used a rope to lower him some food and water. The Air Force, and all of us, can be proud of Bob Purcell's effort to help a friend in need.

DOING WHAT'S RIGHT

It was Christmas 1968 and the Vietnamese had announced that they would receive and distribute Christmas gifts sent by POW families provided that they did not exceed two kilograms. When the guard came to my cell door with a package from my wife, I was overjoyed. But he demanded that I sign a receipt. "No problem," I thought at first, but the receipt stated the following: "I, (fill in the blank), criminal number (fill in the blank), acknowledge receipt of this package." "Whoa," I said, "I'm no criminal; I'm a prisoner of war." Well, I never received the package. I did get a letter, though, from my father. The date had been cut off and several sentences, phrases, and words had been excised with a razor blade. The letter told me of my mother's sudden and unexpected death caused by a brain tumor. The Vietnamese then indicated that I could petition Ho Chi Minh, that nation's leader, to ask for early release. "No thanks," I responded. You've got to do what's right because your conscience will haunt you forever if you don't.

GOD BLESS AMERICA

Irving Berlin

God bless America
Land that I love
Stand beside her, and guide her
Through the night with a light from above.

From the mountains, to the prairies,
To the ocean, white with foam
God bless America
My home sweet home.

God bless America,
Land that I love
Stand beside her, and guide her,
Through the night with a light from above,

From the mountains, to the prairies,
To the ocean, white with foam,
God bless America,
My home sweet home,

God bless America,
My home sweet home.

Major Ira Simpson
U.S. Air Force (Ret.) • WWII • ETO

As a young boy growing up during the Depression years, I was taught by my parents, church leaders, and teachers to have faith in God, my country, and my fellow man. Because of this, my advice for life is: Have faith in God, your nation, and your fellow man. Great faith will help in the search for both success and significance. There is an old adage, "Don't seek to be a great man; seek to be a man of great faith."

FAITH IN GOD

I was born March 11, 1924, in Jackson, Mississippi, attended local schools, and joined the Army Air Corps in November 1942. I received my basic training in Miami Beach, Florida, and then went to James Millikin University in Decatur, Illinois, to complete my cadet training. From there I took my preflight training at Santa Ana Army Air Base in California. I was selected for Navigation Training and completed the school at Hondo Army Air Field, Hondo, Texas. Finally, I was assigned to a B-24 crew in April 1944. In August we were assigned to the 389th Bomb Group in Hethel, England. On my 20th mission, we were shot down over Holland. I parachuted from the aircraft, was captured, and became a prisoner of war.

My faith in God and in answered prayer served me well during the days of my imprisonment in a German prisoner of war camp. I knew that with God's help I would survive the starvation, cruel treatment, and denial of my freedom. I also knew that many people were praying for me and that God answers prayer.

Because of my faith in my country, I was certain that I was not forgotten and that the prisoners would be liberated by our armed forces as soon as they could reach us. I had no doubts that we would be free again.

The willingness of the men in the camp to help others by sharing small amounts of food that were received, assisting those who were ill, and providing companionship sustained my faith in my fellow man. There were many examples of compassion, kindness to others, and friendship too numerous to mention. I know of no other group of men who were so dedicated to those around them.

I have continued to live by this faith during my military and civilian career. I find my faith to be important in my relationship with others and the basis of any success I have achieved. I believe that these principles are ones that will make any life successful and significant.

Ralph Sirianni
WWII • ETO

I live by these three words: pride, respect, attitude. I feel children should be taught at an early age the significance of these three words. If they live by them, they will become good people and good Americans. I also live by the Ten Commandments and respect every person's religious beliefs and practices, whatever they may be.

PRIDE, RESPECT, ATTITUDE

For almost 66 years, I served my country in some capacity. I have had the honor, privilege and opportunity to serve my town as an elected member of the Board of Health and as a town meeting member. On the state level, I was elected to the Massachusetts Legislature for ten years. I served in the United States Army Air Corps as a staff sergeant and as a right waist gunner on a B-17 flying fortress. I have been richly blessed in my 66 years of service, living by the virtues of pride, respect, attitude, and always attempting to live by the Ten Commandments.

Jack Sites
WWII • ETO

My experience as a prisoner of war taught me that the price of freedom is certainly not free, but rather very costly. When faced with life's most trying moments and hardships, surviving and enduring with honor requires character and integrity above reproach. One must have courage at all times when difficult challenges come one's way and in the face of imminent and even great danger.

Companionship, love, and unity are critical elements when dealing with the pain and suffering of these difficult times. I recall seeing this 60 years ago as a POW during an 86-day forced march through Poland and Germany. I watched American POWs, most of whom didn't even know each other, demonstrate great compassion and love for each other. The loyalty and sacrifice made by individuals who stood united during these times demonstrated the great courage and pride these men had in themselves, their country, and their comrades. It made me proud to be a part of the United States Army Air Corps.

Everyday acts of kindness and love help us survive the greatest hardships and trials we endure throughout our lives. It allows us to survive with integrity and gives us the ability to continue on with our journey through life.

Faith, integrity, courage, commitment, persistence, and pride are the foundation, the very cornerstone, upon which this great nation was built.

These characteristics, these qualities, are what make this country "the land of the free and the home of the brave."

———◆◆◆———

THERE IS GOOD IN EVERYONE

I was a ball turret gunner on a B-24 bomber during World War II. On July 26, 1944, while on my 16th mission over Albania, my airplane and crew were shot down by enemy fire. We were captured and held prisoner for more than 10 months. Those 10 months were the longest 10 months of my life. This experience in survival is one that I will never forget. I remember watching my fellow crew members being subjected to terrible beatings while in a Bulgarian prison camp.

One of our crew members was a Jewish officer. During our torture, the members of our crew were asked to sign a document that stated that this crew member (the Jewish officer) had ordered us to kill German women and children. Although we suffered numerous beatings, not one of the crew would sign the document. The horrible conditions and treatment that followed are too painful to discuss. Many of my friends and other servicemen died while held prisoner.

I learned as a prisoner of war to have faith in my God, my family, my country, and my comrades. Even after such a terrible ordeal and seeing how awful one man can be toward another, I still believe that there is something good in everyone. I strive every day to find that good thing in everyone I encounter. The good in people is there; you might have to look deeper in some than in others, but I assure you it is still there. You must have faith in God and faith in each other. Righteousness will prevail.

Edward Slater
Korea

I would offer the following as my advice for life. In life it is important to never give up and to always stand up for what you believe in and what you know is right. If I was asked for spiritual advice it would be, "Have faith in God; and remember, God first, then country, and both above self."

GOD IS FAITHFUL

I was in the 21st infantry regiment of the 24th Division when the Korean War started. We were sent into combat at Osan, Korea, on July 5, 1950, to stem the tide of the advancing North Koreans. My unit was overrun by a horde of North Koreans. I escaped capture for two weeks by hiding in caves, bushes, and ditches in the mountains. Finally, worn out, very hungry and thirsty, I was captured in a village where I had been befriended by an old couple who fed me and gave me water. However, it was possible that they may have called the North Korean soldiers who captured me.

From that point on, my life in Korea was a living hell! I was beaten routinely. I was denied food and water for long periods of time. I was paraded in front of the civilian population for propaganda purposes. I was interrogated, tortured, and suffered through the heat and cold for the next few months. I was almost convinced that God had forgotten me.

After many long hard miles of marching northward on my bleeding and bare feet, we were finally put aboard a train. Unfortunately, the train was shot up by our fighter bombers. As a result the guards went into a frenzy and started machine gunning the prisoners. I fell under the pile. I was wounded, but not badly. The guards poured diesel fuel over us and left us for dead. A friend, Bob, was lying on top of me badly wounded and bleeding on me. (Bob survived because I later brought help to him.) I finally worked my way free and went back down the tracks to the train station where I promptly fell asleep! When I awoke, there was a young boy there who, in pretty good English, said, "Follow me and I will get you food." He said he had learned English from some GIs. He took me to a nearby hut where an old lady fed me. While eating I heard a commotion outside the door. The door suddenly slid open and there stood an angel! This angel was a 6-foot 2-inch Master Sergeant. He took my hand and said, "Let me take you home." So you see, not all angels come equipped with a halo and wings. Some come in the form of Master Sergeants! God had not forgotten me after all!

John Smith
U.S. Air Force (Ret.) • WWII • PTO

Personality, self-confidence, honesty, and morality—the right mixture of these traits will ensure a successful life and career. Treating people with respect and dignity plus developing a work philosophy that will entice people to willingly work for you and with you is a must. You cannot succeed individually—all great leaders are partially judged on their advisors.

Self-confidence is self-explanatory. Believe in and trust yourself above all others. Be willing to trust your own judgment in making decisions. Honesty and morality go hand in hand. These traits are developed during childhood and should be expanded during your lifetime as experience dictates.

SOMEONE WAS LOOKING OUT FOR US

Why did Stalin release us and not the other 7,600? This story was classified until the mid-1990s. I was the navigator on a B-24 bombing the Japanese Kurlie Islands. We were shot down on May 10, 1945 and landed in Kamchatka, Russia. The Soviet Union had yet to join the war with Japan and was technically neutral. However, that did not dissuade them from shooting at us when we tried to land. We were committed to internee status, and my parents back home received the dreaded "Missing in Action" telegram.

As the war progressed, our internment camp grew from 12 to 53. We were later moved across Siberia to a camp near Iran where we were held until the conclusion of the Pacific war. The 53 of us were then released to American control. During the same period, the Soviets took approximately 7600 other Allied personnel who were also moved to Siberia and are still classified as MIA. Why did Stalin release us and not the others? I can only assume that Someone was looking out for us.

William Smith
Korea

I was a young career soldier caught up in combat in North Korea, where I was held captive by the North Korean and Chinese Communists for two and one half years. I survived by the will of God and the prayers of my grandmother. My total faith, mixed with pure stubbornness, gave me the will not to give up.

The long days and the dark nights were spent helping the sick and wounded and gave me little time to think about self. My greatest pain was seeing my buddies die. You wonder, "Why them and not me?" Then you realize that it is in God's will, and He is not yet ready for you.

All who came out of the ordeal came out with integrity, honor, and pride in having done their duty even when it wasn't easy. My code of conduct has always been to try to do what I believe is right, and everything will fall into place. Remember, "All things work together for good to those who love the Lord."

GOD WILL SUSTAIN US

In 1944 at the age of 15, I joined the Army and took my basic training at Camp Joseph T. Robinson, Arkansas. Five months after I entered the Army, my mother called my father who was in the Air Force. My father contacted his commanding officer, the commander then called my commanding officer to inform him that I was not old enough to be in the Army. I was called to the office of the commander and was told that I would have to return home and not to come back until I was 17. In 1947, when I turned 17, I re-enlisted.

After re-enlisting, I was sent to Korea with the occupation force in 1948. In 1950, after two years of service, I was on a ship leaving Japan when the Korean War started. The ship was also carrying many civilians so we returned to the United States. I was reassigned to a new unit, sent to Edgewood Arsenal, Maryland, and then shipped out for Korea. Arriving in Korea in September, I immediately went into combat.

We were attached to the 1st ROK Division (Republic of Korea) and moved north. On the night of November 1, 1950, nine of us were sent to hold a roadblock. There were five Americans and four ROK soldiers. We fought all night and ran out of ammunition. At daybreak we were fighting in hand-to-hand combat. The company was ordered to withdraw, but word never reached us. We realized that we were now fighting not only North Korean soldiers but also Chinese troops who had crossed the border.

That morning at 10:00 a.m. we were overrun and captured. I was wounded and lying on the ground. One of the enemy soldiers pointed his gun at me, preparing to fire, and I began to pray. I still remember saying, "Lord God, don't let him shoot." His weapon misfired. He then moved to my left and shot one of the ROK soldiers. He returned to me and tried to fire the weapon at me, but the gun jammed again. He then directed his weapon to the right and shot the ROK soldier on my right. They killed the two remaining ROK soldiers and then took us Americans captive. At that time I felt that my grandmother was praying for me…it was my first real encounter with God and the power of prayer.

We were tied to each other with telephone wire, and we began to march north. My best guess is that we marched about 25 to 30 nights. During the day we were kept in caves and periodically in farm houses. When we reached the POW compound, we found the conditions were primitive. To make the situation worse, many soldiers were wearing summer uniforms, and men died from exposure and starvation. Some of the guards were sadistic, and the treatment was horrible. I spent time in the hole as punishment for resisting the indoctrination of my Communist captors. I spent four months in solitary confinement in the basement vault of a bank.

We were able to determine how things were going on the front by the way the guards acted and reacted. If we were on the offensive, the cruelty of the guards increased, and the beating and punishment became more severe. I always prayed when they were beating me. I would tell the guard that my God was everywhere, and He knew what was happening to me and what they were doing to me.

We were frequently forced to squat or sit on the frozen ground for punishment when it was 40-50 degrees below zero. We had to listen to their propaganda lectures for 8-10 hours. Another form of punishment was to make us stand on the ice of the frozen Yalu river. I had to do this several times, one time for eight hours. To keep my mind occupied, I would pray and try to remember Bible verses that I learned as a child. I found great comfort in prayer.

God saved me many times during the two and a half years that I spent as a POW in North Korea. One day, however, stands out above all others. We were sitting outside during another indoctrination lecture. One of the guards was behind us when I made a comment to my friend sitting beside me. The guard grabbed me and began kicking and pulling me out in front of the formation. The lecture was being given by a dedicated Communist named Comrade Lin. We called him "The Screaming Skull." He told me, "I can kill you now, so kneel and pray to me not to shoot you." A peace came over me, and I responded, "My faith says I pray to no man." I figured that I was a dead man, but I still had total peace. Two of my buddies rushed forward, risking their own lives, and told Mr. Lin not to pay any attention to me because I was sick. Only God knows why Mr. Lin did not have me shot.

I returned home in April 1953. In August I met a wonderful girl and we were married in December 1955. We have one daughter and two wonderful granddaughters. I pray daily that whatever task God has for me to do, I will be capable of it. We must live life with courage, hope, and determination in the knowledge that God will sustain us, and He is always there when we need Him.

POW/MIA STATISTICS

	WWI	WWII	Korea	Vietnam	Gulf	Somalia
Captured or interned	4,120	130,201	7,140	744	23	1
Died in captivity	147	14,072	2,701	84	0	0

TOTAL ALL WARS:

Captured/interned	142,257
Died in captivity	17,034

At this time there are approximately 36,000 living American Ex-Prisoners of War. There are 89,000 Americans listed as MIA.

Vice Admiral James Stockdale
U.S. Navy (Ret.) • Vietnam
Medal of Honor

One's integrity can give a person something to rely on when perspectives seem to blur, when rules and principles seem to waver, and when we're faced with hard choices between right and wrong. A clear conscience is one's only protection.

CITATION

For conspicuous gallantry and intrepidity at the risk of his life above and beyond the call of duty while senior naval officer in the Prisoner of War camps of North Vietnam.

Recognized by his captors as the leader in the Prisoners of War resistance to interrogation and in their refusal to participate in propaganda exploitation, Rear Adm. Stockdale was singled out for interrogation and attendant torture after he was detected in a covert communications attempt. Sensing the start of another purge, and aware that his earlier efforts at self-disfiguration to dissuade his captors from exploiting him for propaganda purposes had resulted in cruel and agonizing punishment, Rear Adm. Stockdale resolved to make himself a symbol of resistance regardless of personal sacrifice. He deliberately inflicted a near-mortal wound to his person in order to convince his captors of his willingness to give up his life rather than capitulate. He was subsequently discovered and revived by the

North Vietnamese who, convinced of his indomitable spirit, abated in their employment of excessive harassment and torture toward all of the Prisoners of War.

By his heroic action, at great peril to himself, he earned the everlasting gratitude of his fellow prisoners and of his country. Rear Adm. Stockdale's valiant leadership and extraordinary courage in a hostile environment sustain and enhance the finest traditions of the U.S. Naval Service.

ALL THINGS WORK TOGETHER FOR GOOD

Many years ago I toured the Old Yuma Territorial Prison with my two oldest sons. Their boyish reactions to the filthy cells used for solitary confinement were predictable. A combination of wonderment and horror was on their faces as they looked at the old, metal leg irons in the small, windowless cells. I told the boys that the days of the old West, desperadoes, and jails like these were gone forever.

Little did I know that within a few years I would find myself in an old French-built prison now known to many as the Hanoi Hilton. One part of the jail I was in was called Alcatraz. I was one of 11 Americans incarcerated in the small, windowless cells.

In a letter to my wife and family dated February 3, 1966, I wrote, "I pray a good deal. Every night I remember each of you individually, and I know you do the same for me. I live for the day of our reunion, which I suppose will be after the war is over. I have no idea how that is working itself out. Let us think positively and remember the Scripture, 'All things work together for good to those who love and serve the Lord.'"

My time as a POW taught me to love God completely and hopefully serve Him better. The experience is one that I will never forget; I am also a better man because of it.

Colonel James Stone
U.S. Army (Ret.) • Korea
Medal of Honor

We should be forever grateful that we are citizens of the greatest nation on earth. No other country can provide you with the world's highest living standard and the many freedoms that all of us enjoy in our daily lives.

Perhaps, sometime in your life, you might be asked to serve your nation or serve in the Armed Forces of the United States. Please do not hesitate—serve with pride, dignity, and honor.

CITATION

1st Lt. Stone distinguished himself by conspicuous gallantry and indomitable courage above and beyond the call of duty in action against the enemy.

When his platoon, holding a vital outpost position, was attacked by overwhelming Chinese forces, 1st Lt. Stone stood erect and exposed to the terrific enemy fire calmly directed his men in the defense. A defensive flame-thrower failing to function, he personally moved to its location, further exposing himself, and personally repaired the weapon. Throughout a second attack, 1st Lt. Stone, though painfully wounded, personally carried the only remaining light machine gun from place to place in the position in order to bring fire upon the Chinese advancing from two directions.

Throughout, he continued to encourage and direct his depleted platoon in its hopeless defense. Although again wounded, he continued the fight with his carbine, still exposing himself as an example to his men. When this final overwhelming assault swept over the platoon's position, his voice could still be heard faintly urging his men to carry on, until he lost consciousness. Only because of this officer's driving spirit and heroic action was the platoon emboldened to make its brave but hopeless last ditch stand.

Clifford Stumpf
WWII • ETO

If I were to offer my advice for life it would be: Live by the Golden Rule. Always treat people the way you would like to be treated. I would also encourage people to have faith in God and to believe in prayer. As a POW, I always knew my mother and my family were praying for me.

THE SANDWICH

My service with the armed forces took me to both the Pacific and the European theaters of war. I firmly believe my faith in God and a strong will to live brought me through a terrible ordeal. I was in the 106th Division that was virtually wiped out in the Battle of the Bulge. After a three-day battle in an encirclement, I was captured on December 19, 1944, one of the coldest winters on record. I did not remove my clothes for six months.

As a POW I was under an entirely different command. There were no good assignments, however some of the areas of confinement were better than others. My belief was that if the good Lord allowed you to come home, then that was the best assignment for you.

We were transferred often by rail in boxcars. Cold and hunger were always with us. After our arrival at one location, we were sent out on different work details: to farms, mines, factories, and any place where labor was needed. I was one of 100 men sent to the city of Dresden, Germany. Dresden was declared an open city and appeared to be a safe place. That all changed when the German Army began to move war materiel into the city.

I had to work on trolley freight cars, delivering freight throughout the city. One day after a bombing, the trolley tracks were damaged and had to be repaired before we could return to our camp. We noticed a damaged German home nearby. While we were waiting for repair, five of us were allowed to help the family straighten up their home. When we were ready to leave, this family risked their lives by leaving each of us a sandwich by a stack of boards. We were so starved that the memory of this sandwich has remained with me all of my life.

A few days later, bombings left Dresden almost completely destroyed. I have often wondered if that family survived. I have questioned what I would have done if I had been in their situation. This experience instilled in me a lesson taught in the Bible: Do good, if you can, to the person you believe might be your enemy. In this instance, an enemy gave a cold and hungry American soldier a sandwich which I believe helped to revive my faith and hope to live and to be able to return home to the United States of America.

Wright Swanay
WWII • ETO

I believe that my experience as a prisoner of war in Germany during World War II instilled in me a sense of duty that has motivated me all my life. The experience inspired me to live a life of loyalty and service—to my family, to my comrades, to my country, and to my God.

I am the last of my family. Fondly I recall the family ties and the sacrifices that helped us through the Depression, through World War II, and through the years that followed. It fell on me to bury them all and settle their affairs. I have few regrets, a million rich and happy memories, and a duty to represent them well to the generations that will follow us.

For many years now I have served as a Veterans' Service Officer at the local, state, and national level, helping my comrades gain benefits to which they were entitled. This has brought me great satisfaction and great reward.

I served my country when called upon in WWII. Unlike Nathan Hale of Revolutionary War fame, I spoke no great words as a POW, just the required name, rank, and service number.

In serving others, I feel I have served my Creator. My creed is found in the book of Micah in the Old Testament, chapter 6, verse 8, "...what doth the Lord require of thee, but to do justly, and to love mercy, and to walk humbly with thy God."

SEASON OF HOPE

The first day of April 1945 was a Sunday. It was April Fools' Day, my birthday, and Easter Sunday. The All Fools Day didn't concern me at all, but I was very conscious that it was my birthday. I observed that Easter by attending a sunrise service, the sun coming up on a bright but chilly day.

I was a prisoner of war in Nuremberg, Germany, Stalag XIIID. I had been a prisoner of war since July 2, 1944, when my plane was shot down over Budapest, Hungary, on my 39th mission. After my capture, I was interned in Stalag Luft III, the famous Luftwaffe camp for captured allied flying officers, the scene of the now famous prisoner of war movie, *The Great Escape*. In late January 1945, I was moved from the camp by foot and then by train to Nuremberg.

On a scale of one to ten, with ten being the best, the Nuremberg camp was a zero. As a POW, I had experienced crowded, filthy living quarters, poor sanitation, cold, hunger, loneliness, boredom, despair, solitary confinement, and bombings by our own planes during both the day and the night. It was a miserable existence, and I was so tired, so fatigued, and so discouraged.

It was announced on the previous day, at the evening count, that Padre MacDonald, a Scottish Chaplain, would hold an Easter Sunrise Service the next morning in the northeast corner of the compound. We gathered under a guard tower beside the barbed wire fence that surrounded the camp. The Padre spoke with a strong Scottish brogue, with such an accent that I could hardly understand his words. Nevertheless, I knew the meaning of Easter, and I could appreciate what he was saying.

I was overwhelmed by the fact that it was Easter and my birthday and I was a POW. I couldn't dismiss it lightly as if it was of no consequence. I was sure there was a meaning in it for me. Easter, of course, means the resurrection of Jesus Christ. Dare I hope that this was a sign, perhaps a promise, that I might also be delivered from the terrible circumstance that I was in? I was humbled by the thought and the possibility.

Those were my thoughts as the Padre spoke. Even in that miserable camp, it was a beautiful service. It was too early for the bombers. We were a quiet group, deadly serious in our Easter worship. I left the service rewarded, my despair melting away, and I had hopes for a better day. I felt that I had been given a promise of better days to come. Thinking about that, I felt a surge of hope, a feeling that I had not experienced for a very long time.

Four weeks later to the day, after a forced march for 17 days covering 95 miles, I was in another camp, Stalag VIIA in Moosberg. I watched one of General Patton's tanks roll over the front gate and crash into the camp. Moments later, the German flag was replaced by the Stars and Stripes. The day I had hoped and prayed for had arrived. I can't describe my feelings. Looking at our flag, I have never been more proud of my country than I was at that moment. My country had not forgotten us. It gave freedom to me and thousands of others in the camp, not just Americans, but many soldiers from other nations of the world. A swift return to my family lay ahead, and I had much to look forward to.

Upon my return home, I discovered that my family had believed that I was killed in action. But there I stood, as if back from the dead, just like the Resurrection. The promise had been kept. Now as I look back on my most memorable Easter and the days that followed, it strengthens my belief in God and my belief in what the angel told the women at the tomb, "He is not here; He is risen."

Those days in April, so long ago now, are my greatest season of hope. I will never forget them and thank the good Lord for the memory of it all. My prisoner of war experience was not a loss. I came through the experience with a greater love for my country and stronger faith in God!

THE BATAAN DEATH MARCH

Approximately 70,000 Filipino and US soldiers commanded by LTG Jonathan Wainwright, formally surrendered to the Japanese on April 9, 1942. Due to a shortage of trucks, the captives were forced to march, beginning the following day, about 100 kilometers north to Nueva Ecija to Camp O'Donnell, a prison camp.

As the march began, the prisoners were beaten randomly and were denied both food and water for days. Those who fell behind were executed; some were shot while others were beheaded or bayoneted. Although no one knows for sure how many died or how many survived the Death March, it is believed approximately 54,000 finally reached Camp O'Donnell.

Captain Charles Nels Tanner
U.S. Navy • Vietnam

Several truths of life were driven home to me during my six and a half years as a POW in North Vietnam:

1. No man is perfect. Perfect or not, he must continue to do his very best.
2. Without God's help, real victory for a man is impossible.
3. To get God's help, you must ask for it. In turn, you must provide help to your fellow man.
4. The love of your fellow man is vital to life.
5. Men cannot lead successfully without proving they are willing to follow.

Although I received most of these truths as a child, they had been put aside and taken for granted until the test of my life was staring me in the face. All this took only a split second, after many years of trust in my personal skills and faith in the technology of man. All this has nothing to do with the Vietnam War—it could have happened anywhere, anytime. Do not wait for the revelation. It could easily be too late!

THE LORD'S PRAYER

I doubt this experience is much different than most Christian's. The Sunday morning that Ross Terry and I were shot down over North Vietnam was a brilliantly sunny day. As soon as my senses recovered from the violent ejection sequence, I looked up at the parachute canopy and saw that it was intact. Without thinking, I began the Lord's Prayer and I found that I was praying it with new meaning. Needless to say, freedom ended just a few minutes later.

In all the days of the six and a half years in Hanoi, that prayer became the mainstay of my evening prayers. I had learned to pray again.

Colonel Leo Thorsness
U.S. Air Force (Ret.) • Vietnam
Medal of Honor

While a POW in Hanoi for six years, I put into conscious thinking a "plan for life." My formula is very basic. It is this: Life = Goals + Commitments + Plans. My definition of life is living a full, productive Christian life.

GOALS: Goals take a lot of deep thinking. I'm talking about having two or three major goals in life. For most, that includes the spiritual life. Also, most will include family, security, and success. Success, unfortunately, is often measured in dollars instead of integrity.

COMMITMENTS: These are the hardest as they must come from the heart and are life-changing. A simple example is a goal to be healthy. In essence, that requires exercising more and eating less and better—a struggle every day for many people. Likewise, a commitment to live as Christ wants us to live is a major change for the majority of us. Commitments are hard to keep!

PLANS: Plans are the easy part. If you keep your commitments, the plans fall into place.

For much of my time as a POW and in my years since release from Hanoi in 1973, this simple formula has served me well.

CITATION

For conspicuous gallantry and intrepidity in action at the risk of his life above and beyond the call of duty. As pilot of an F-105 aircraft, Lt. Col. Thorsness was on a surface-to-air missile suppression mission over North Vietnam. Lt. Col. Thorsness and his wingman attacked and silenced a surface-to-air missile site with air-to-ground missiles, and then destroyed a second surface-to-air missile site with bombs. In the attack on the second missile site, Lt. Col. Thorsness' wingman was shot down by intensive antiaircraft fire, and the 2 crewmembers abandoned their aircraft. Lt. Col. Thorsness circled the descending parachutes to keep the crewmembers in sight and relay their position to the Search and Rescue Center.

During this maneuver, a MIG-17 was sighted in the area. Lt. Col. Thorsness immediately initiated an attack and destroyed the MIG. Because his aircraft was low on fuel, he was forced to depart the area in search of a tanker. Upon being advised that 2 helicopters were orbiting over the downed crew's position and that there were hostile MIGs in the area posing a serious threat to the helicopters, Lt. Col. Thorsness, despite his low fuel condition, decided to return alone through a hostile environment of surface-to-air missile and antiaircraft defenses to the downed crew's position.

As he approached the area, he spotted 4 MIG-17 aircraft and immediately initiated an attack on the MIGs, damaging 1 and driving the others away from the rescue scene. When it became apparent that an aircraft in the area was critically low on fuel and the crew would have to abandon the aircraft unless they could reach a tanker, Lt. Col. Thorsness, although critically short on fuel himself, helped to avert further possible loss of life and a friendly aircraft by recovering at a forward operating base, thus allowing the aircraft in emergency fuel condition to refuel safely.

Lt. Col. Thorsness' extraordinary heroism, self-sacrifice, and personal bravery involving conspicuous risk of life were in the highest traditions of the military service, and have reflected great credit upon himself and the U.S. Air Force.

PEOPLE OR TRUCKS

I taxied with two F-105 fighters to the end of the runway at Takhli, Thailand, in January 1967. I had about 50 Wild Weasel missions over North Vietnam in my assigned mission to seek out and destroy Surface to Air Missile (SAM) sites.

We had the standard wait at the end of the runway while the ground crews armed our guns, bombs, and air-to-ground missiles. The wait was especially long as several aircraft were landing. As we waited to take the runway, my backseater and I talked about the Thai peasants who were working at the end of the runway. It seemed the women were doing most of the work while the men were hunkering and smoking cigarettes. We couldn't hear the conversation, of course, but it was obvious that none were working too hard and most of them were having a good time as they laughed, pointed, and exchanged lots of banter. Harry, my backseater, and I commented that it was nice they were enjoying life.

Normally all North Vietnamese SAMs were kept within 100 miles of Hanoi or so. Occasionally they would sneak one down by the DMZ to get a shot at a B-52 or refueling tanker. There were overnight reports from electronic intelligence aircraft that the North Vietnamese may have sneaked a SAM just north of the DMZ. Our early morning mission was to see if it was there and destroy it.

My wingman and I made the 40-minute flight to the southern part of North Vietnam. Several times we crisscrossed the narrow span of North Vietnam between Laos and the Gulf of Tonkin without picking up any electronic signals of the SAM's radar.

We stayed at least 10,000 feet above a low, solid cloud cover so if they quickly launched a SAM, we would have time to see and out-maneuver it. We saw no SAMs and heard no signals and were getting close to our low fuel depart time. Just then, faster than I'd ever seen before, the solid but thin, low cloud layer quickly burned off from the early morning sun. I dropped down to about 5,000 feet for a better visual inspection of the suspected SAM site. What I saw instead were hundreds of North Vietnamese working to repair the previous day's bomb damage to Highway 1, the North Vietnamese main route for supplies from Hanoi to the South. The workers were out in the open, a perfect target for my CBU bombs. (CBUs are mother bombs that, when dropped, have a shell

262

that opens and about a thousand hand-grenade-sized bomblets spew out and explode when hitting the ground. CBUs are perfect weapons for thin-skinned things like missiles and people.)

It was nearly time to head home, and we found a perfectly legitimate target—North Vietnamese helping get supplies to their troops in South Vietnam to fight and kill Americans. I looked over the area and about a mile north of the peasants were several trucks and busses—obviously transport for the workers.

I made a radio call, "Cadillac two, afterburner now; go bomb mode." I pulled my nose up and climbed for 18,000 feet to roll on a bomb run. In the few seconds it took to climb, my wingman called, "Cadillac lead, what's the target?"

We had two legitimate targets—people or trucks—and we had the right weapons for either. While reaching for 18,000 feet, the image of happy Thai workers we had watched just an hour ago flashed in my mind. Here were similar people, living under communism, forced to work in an open area filling bomb craters and fearing they were about to be bombed. My mind said the best target was the peasants; my heart said it was the trucks. The Thai peasants' image stayed in my mind. The entire thought process lasted the few seconds I had before deciding the target: people or trucks.

As vividly as if it were yesterday, I recall turning my head and looking at my left shoulder. There sat Jesus Christ. I asked, "People or trucks?" As quickly as I asked, He answered, "Trucks."

As we rolled over inverted and started pulling our nose earthward into a bomb run, I called, "Cadillac two, we hit the trucks!"

Charles Towne
WWII • PTO
Past National Commander
American Ex-POW Association 1968-1969

My motto for life is: Don't ever give up! We exist to help those who cannot help themselves. Always remember there is an angel watching over you!

GOD WAS WATCHING OUT FOR ME

I joined the Army National Guard in 1937 and was assigned to a station hospital in the Philippines. Most of the time I worked as a medic in the field. I became a Japanese prisoner of war in 1942. I was one of those unfortunate captives on the "Hellship" Oryoku Maru when it was bombed by aircraft from the USS Hornet. More than 1600 prisoners were on the ship when it headed for Japan. The first attack killed at least 300 prisoners. Those of us who survived were re-assembled at San Fernando La Union, Philippine Islands and placed on board two more Hellships, the Enoura Maru and the Brazil Maru.

The POWs suffered inhuman treatment, hunger, thirst, and unbelievable filth that pervaded the holds of the ships. Men were dying everyday. On December 31, New Year's Eve, we reached Takao, Formosa. The Japanese guards celebrated the New Year by leaving the POWs to fend for themselves for four days. The small amount of food and water was not adequate to sustain life and more men died.

On January 9th, aircraft, again from the USS Hornet, attacked the Enoura Maru. After the attack, less than 1,000 POWs had survived the trip to Japan. By the end of the war, only 400 of the original 1600 men were still alive.

I was listed as MIA for the first 18 months of my captivity. Toward the end of the war, I was in a hospital in Korea with a severe infection in my spine. When the war ended, I shipped back to Manila for further hospitalization. I survived the experience only because God was watching out for me.

Merle "Gil" Turley
WWII • ETO

The motto of the American ex-POW is "Freedom is not free." This one small statement is the most forgotten, ignored, and unappreciated grouping of words by the people of the United States today. Think of Memorial Day—how many people remember why we really have this day on our calendar? Then, there is Veteran's Day. Who attends the parades? On National POW Day, who thanks a veteran or ex-POW for their sacrifice so everyone can enjoy the freedom they have in this country?

A common saying of the ex-POW is "Freedom, ask us." This is truly a question we can answer. Not only were we combat veterans, but we have gone one step further. Our freedom was taken from us, we were humiliated, starved, beaten, lost our self-esteem, experienced loneliness, and lost all the benefits of freedom. All we had to fight this experience was our faith. We had faith that our country would liberate us. We had faith that our families would remember and pray for us. Last but not least, we had faith in a supreme being and that He was looking after us and would liberate us from this trial. All this the POWs kept bottled up within themselves after we were liberated until the past few years because we felt that no one would believe our experiences. We did not seek sympathy. We only wanted to be recognized as the defenders of freedom, the freedom we all enjoy today. Together we all must have faith in country, family, friends, God, and ourselves.

FAITH

I entered the Army Air Force in February of 1943 and was assigned to the 44th Bomb Group and the 506th Squadron. I was cross-trained as a nose gunner, bombardier, and navigator on a B-24 Liberator bomber. On our ninth mission on August 12, 1944, we were shot down over France. Three in our crew were killed. Of the seven who survived, five were captured by the Germans but two escaped.

I was a prisoner of war at Stalag Luft I in Barth. The camp was liberated by the Russians. Apparently a Russian general ordered the POWs to begin marching to Russia. Our commander, Colonel Hubert Zenke, a captured P-51 pilot and Fighter Group Leader, refused to obey the order. He was able to make contact with the British, and eventually Field Marshall Montgomery gave an order that the allied POWs at Stalag Luft I were to remain until they could be repatriated to their own country.

I am convinced that Colonel Zenke saved our lives. Most of us were too weak to have endured a forced march to Russia. After the war, we also found out that many allied servicemen in Russia never returned. I credit my survival to the prayers of people across the United States and to the prayers of my family.

Over the years I have become involved with speaking to military personnel. As an Ex-POW, I believe the question that I am most frequently asked is, "How did you survive, and what was the most important thing that made it possible for you to survive?" My answer has always been the same over all these years. The answer is faith. You must have faith: faith in your country, your family, and God. Without faith and without hope, you will not make it home.

Stanley Tyron
WWII • ETO

The advice for life that I would give is: Never give up and always trust in God! Everyone needs to realize that they set an example for someone. It is so very important to be the best example that you can be. The lives of young people can be changed forever by seeing people do what is right.

When someone is in need, offer them help; live by the Golden Rule, and do what Jesus told us to do—love one another.

FLY HIGH, MY EAGLE SON

March 18, 1945, I was flying a strafing mission out of Italy at a marshalling yard near Vienna, Austria. On my first run I targeted a steam engine and several boxcars trying to get into a tunnel. I was able to hit the train, but as I pulled away and to the left, I received a direct hit from antiaircraft fire and lost oil pressure immediately. I gained as much altitude as I could before the engine quit. Left with only one option, I bailed out. The descent was too quick, and I hit the ground hard. The pain from my ankles caused me to black out. When I regained consciousness, four German soldiers where kicking me and pounding me with their rifle butts, and two civilians were hitting me with large sticks about my head and neck. After they finished, they allowed me to get up. They made me carry my parachute and life raft to a village about two miles away. There they put me in a local jail. The elderly couple that ran the jail gave me water and a towel to clean my wounds, and later that evening they fed me cabbage and potatoes. That was my last meal for three days. Thus began my time as a prisoner of war.

From the time I started high school, I was sure that I wanted to be an officer and a pilot in the United States military. My father was originally from Denmark, having come to the United States in the early 1900s. When WWI started, he wanted to help so he joined the Army, became a bugler, and eventually was able to obtain his citizenship. He met my mother in Baltimore, Maryland, and they married in 1918. I was born in 1921.

I was blessed to have a father who was a wonderful moral compass. By the time I was 12, I told him that I wanted to be a Boy Scout. He was a member of the American Legion, and he convinced the other members that the Legion should sponsor a Scout Troop. I was thrilled about being a scout and was glad to encourage other boys to join the troop. We lived in a low-income neighborhood, and the discipline, study, and values of scouting were a big part of our lives. I was fortunate to rise through the ranks and attain the rank of an Eagle Scout.

The mayor of Kansas City was a dedicated advocate of scouting, and he helped organize a meeting where all those who attained the rank of Eagle Scout would be recognized. The meeting was held in the old Kansas City Auditorium. As we entered the auditorium, each scout was given a small box of wooden matches. When the meeting started, we were all called to attention. The Mayor then gave a wonderful speech. When he concluded, he told each of us to take a match out of the box. When everyone had a match in their hands, they turned the lights out. It was black as night in the large auditorium. The Mayor then told us to light a match, and the entire auditorium seemed to light up. He explained that every one of us could be a light to the world and that with our combined light, we could light the darkness. Then he offered a prayer and led everyone in singing the National Anthem. The ceremony concluded when the mother of each Eagle Scout pinned the new rank and medal on their son.

In every letter that my mother ever sent me, she closed with the words: "Fly high, my Eagle son." In life we can choose to fly with the eagles. There is an old saying, "It's hard to be an eagle if you surround yourself with a bunch of turkeys." I was blessed to be able to achieve my dreams, to be an Eagle Scout, to become a Army fighter pilot, and to serve my nation. Oddly enough, the insignia for my Squadron was an eagle.

In Isaiah 40:31 we read, "But they that wait upon the Lord shall renew their strength; they shall mount up with wings as eagles; they shall run, and not be weary; and they shall walk, and not faint." Lord, help me to wait!

THE DEATH MARCH
ACROSS GERMANY

There were approximately 9,000-10,000 POWs at Stalag Luft IV. Near the end of the war and as the advancing front neared, the order for the evacuation of the sick and wounded was given. By February 6, 1945, the remaining POWs set out on foot. The estimated total was about 6,000 POWs who were broken down into groups of 250-300. They marched four or five abreast. At night, if they were lucky, they slept in barns. The barns would be so crowded that some had to sleep standing up. When no shelter was available, they would have to sleep in the open.

From the beginning to end, the march spanned 86 days and an estimated 600 miles. Many of the survivors went from an average of 150 pounds to 90 pounds. Of those who survived, many suffered from injuries and illnesses for the remainder of their lives. Estimates are that as many as 1,300 died on the march.

Chief Master Sergeant
Maynard "Doc" Unger
U.S. Air Force (Ret.) • WWII • ETO

The Lord spared my life, and I am constantly reminding myself that He must have something in mind for me. I truly believe He has directed my life. I certainly didn't plan it.

It just happened. My faith in God brought me through WWII, including 22 months in a German prisoner of war experience. Did it change me? Certainly, and for the best! I now have a high level of patriotism, God-given talent, and a desire to serve others. My faith, confidence, reliability, and reasonably good health have allowed me to be placed in positions of leadership ever since my POW experience. In all these opportunities, I have striven to do my best. I hope to be remembered for service to God, my family, and others.

HE WATCHES OVER ME

I was born in Berlin Heights, Ohio. At that time kids were allowed to roam and play almost everywhere without supervision. It was understood and generally accepted that any adult could scold you, so in a sense, everyone in the community helped raise the children. There were some dangers, like playing in the nearby ravine, along the railroad tracks, and the rock quarry, but these places were also great areas in which to play. I guess even then God must have been looking out for me.

As I reflect on and remember my childhood, I remember Sunday school and church were always part of my life. My mother always made sure that both my brother and I participated. One of my prized possessions is a book of Bible stories given to me by my mother on my first birthday. I had the book cover rebound to preserve it and the note that she wrote to me on my first birthday. My mother died when I was nine years old. After her death, my grandmother helped raise me. Sunday school and church were also part of my grandmother's life, and again, were considered a must for me as well. Mr. Albert Friedenstein was my Sunday school teacher during high school. He was a wonderful man and a great role model for young men. He lived to be 100 years old. With his spiritual mentoring and training, I left for the military and WWII.

During the war I was a radio operator on a bomber flying out of England. The day I flew my first mission, a bomb exploded in a plane while we were still on the ground. The explosion killed 26 men. The 381st Bomb Group was not off to a very good start. I successfully completed 12 missions, but on the 13th mission, my luck ran out...or did it?

I was assigned to the 534th Squadron. Five of the six bombers were shot down on the same day, August 17, 1943. Four of these bombers crashed in enemy territory, and one crashed in the English Channel. The target that day was a ball-bearing factory in Schweinfurt, Germany. This was the deepest penetration into enemy territory up to that period. The flak from the anti-aircraft guns literally filled the sky, as did German fighters. It seemed the German fighters were everywhere. We put up a good fight against the fighters, but our aircraft was eventually damaged so severely that it was crippled and on fire. Our pilot had no choice; it was either crash or jump. He ordered the crew to jump.

I have called on God for help many times in my life, none surpassing

273

my prayer to Him following the experience of being shot down and becoming a POW. To this day and for whatever reason, I felt a special protection from Almighty God during the battle, when our plane was hit, and during my life-saving parachute jump. When I hit the ground and landed, my first thoughts and actions were directed toward saving my life. Even though I was captured almost immediately, I still felt joy and thanked God for allowing me to survive. I spent my first week of captivity alone, in solitary confinement. I wondered what had happened to the rest of my crew and if they had survived. I also wondered what was going to happen to me and this allowed me a lot of time to talk to God and to pray.

After my first week of isolation, I was reunited with other surviving airmen; some were members of my crew. For the next 21 months, despite harsh conditions, poor nutrition, and forced marches, I felt fortunate and even blessed to be with friends that I knew. For a short period we had a church building in our camp. The German guards found an escape tunnel that was being dug under the church so the Germans destroyed the building. Religious services and activities continued, and I was able to participate.

I am convinced that my entire life was changed as a result of my experience as a prisoner of war. I believe that God has continued to direct my life, He has directed my steps, and He has blessed me with reasonably good health to do His bidding. I have had the opportunity to serve and to lead in many positions. After the war I took advantage of the GI Bill and went to college. This allowed me the opportunity to serve in my church, my community, and in scouting and veterans' organizations.

I tell people to live by the Ten Commandments. I truly believe the teachings of Jesus Christ and His promise of life after our time on earth. I pray with the confidence that God knows what is best for me and I put everything in His hands. Jesus said, "Don't worry." I try to live by those words.

HELLSHIPS

The name "Hellship" is derived from the absolute horror, abuse, and atrocities associated with the voyage on these ships. Literally hundreds of Hellships carried thousands of POWs and internees to Japan and other destinations under the control of the Japanese. Thousands of POWs and internees were killed or died during these voyages. Hellships departed the Philippines as early as January 1942, and were known to have carried captives as late as July 1945. No one will ever know exactly how many individuals were killed or died on these ships. Many Hellships were unknowingly sunk by allied air and sea forces raising the death toll of those imprisoned on the ships.

INTERNEES

It is estimated that as many as 300,000 POWs and internees were held by the Japanese during WWII. The greatest number of these individuals were taken captive in Java, Singapore, Sumatra, and the Philippines. Prisoners were often transferred from one prison to another for labor requirements of the Japanese. The total number of those who died in captivity or were killed is unknown.

John Vennink
WWII • ETO

Our first commitment should be to have faith and trust in God. The second is to live by the Golden Rule. In life you should also always do what is right. No matter what you do, whether at work or wherever you are, someone is watching. You have the choice to set a good example or a bad one.

I would also stress the importance of education and, more importantly, a love of learning. Whether you are in school, have completed your education, or are working at your occupation, continue to learn. Keep up with current events and conduct yourself in a manner that helps our nation and others to have a better life.

THERE IS A GOD

I entered the Army Air Corps in June 1941. I was assigned to the 12th Bomb Group of the 81st Squadron. In July 1942, I left the United States and set foot on four continents in less than one month. On our fourth mission, our plane was hit by flak. The plane caught fire, and I injured my back when I bailed out.

I do not regret my two and a half years as a POW, first, because I survived and second, due to my back injuries, my only recreation was reading. The camp I was in had a library, and the library had books that I would have never been able to read had I not been a POW. I read two different books by the Russian scientists, Immanuel Velikovsky. Initially he set out to prove there was no God, but he ended up believing there was a Supreme Being who created life.

Growing up in a family that encouraged learning and reading made it easy for me to read as a youth, as a prisoner, and even now at 88 years of age. I continue to read and enjoy learning. Children today seem to be at a disadvantage because they watch so much television and play computer games, allowing little time to read. More than 2,400 years ago the Greek philosopher, physician, and poet, Aristotle, wrote a play depicting the downfall of democracy and freedom of spirit (the press). What he wrote then seems to be happening now. Part of the problem is certainly related to the fact that our politicians are no longer statesmen, and part of the problem is we have abandoned our love of learning.

Emilio "Vince" Vizachero, Jr.
WWII • ETO

Never, never give up! Always be honest. It is often said, "Honesty is not only the best policy, it is the *only* policy." During the time I grew up, many people were not able to obtain a high school education, let alone an advanced education. I would encourage everyone to continue in school and obtain the greatest level of education that you can.

My advice about faith would be: Reach out every day for Jesus Christ and His guidance.

Remember that there is more to life than monetary gain. Live by the Golden Rule, treating others the way you want to be treated, and always, always, trust in God.

WILD DAISIES—THE HOPE TO SURVIVE

My code of conduct as an American POW in WWII was as follows: To our captors we gave only our name, rank and service number. When our captors ordered us to do forced labor at gunpoint, we did so. When our captors ordered us to make propaganda statements or be subjected to torture, we steadfastly refused. When our captors offered us extra food and water if we would denounce our country, we told them we would rather die first. We American POWs were the spirit of America. Our absolute dedication to God gave us hope and courage to endure the pain and suffering. When Jesus Christ my Savior was at the door, I didn't hesitate to open it. I wrote the following poem as a POW in Augsburg, Germany. The long and painful months as a German POW changed my life forever, but God gave me the courage to endure the suffering:

> Looking through the barbed wire fence
> at those wild daisies, oh, how I envy such freedom!
>
> Trying to reach through the fence
> to pick a handful,
> but they evaded my clutching hand.
>
> It had to be God's way,
> giving me hope and faith to survive.
> So when droplets of tears come to your eyes,
> just clutch a handful of God's wild daisies.

Glenn Wade
WWII • ETO

I was a navigator in World War II. I grew up in the depth of the Depression, and being a Christian certainly gave me strength to take whatever the Germans handed me. I was a POW in Germany for more than 27 months. Padre McDonald always preached that God was not responsible for the predicament we were in, and that God and Jesus would see us through.

We needed to have courage and faith and to be an honorable servant to the USA. Our attitude and how we spent our time were very important in surviving such a difficult ordeal. We always tried to believe we would make it through. We had good training, and we were disciplined to do whatever we needed to do. We spent our time improving our minds and keeping physically strong, having classes, reading, arts, and competitive sports.

THE GUARDIAN ANGEL

As a young POW in Stalag Luft III, I carried hundreds of bags of sand and dirt hidden inside my pant legs. As I walked across the compound, I would pull a string and the dirt would fall to the ground. The dirt came from the tunnel that was being dug and would later become known by the 1963 movie starring James Garner and Steve McQueen as *The Great Escape*. Days before the escape, the Germans decided to move the American troops to another barracks and separate the British and the Americans. The men who escaped were from barracks 104, and the Americans were moved to barracks 105. Of the 79 men who escaped, only a few made it to freedom. Fifty of the men were recaptured and executed by the Germans.

I volunteered for the Army Air Force in September 1941. Part of my training was at Kelly Field in Texas. In 1943, at age 25, I was a navigator of a B-17, flying my eighth mission when we were shot down by a German Fighter. When I bailed out of the plane and pulled my ripcord, nothing happened. I thought, *This is it. I'm going to die.* Somehow the parachute finally deployed and opened. To this day I believe my guardian angel saved my life, and I also believe that my guardian angel was with me during my entire experience as a POW.

After my capture I was taken by train to Bremen, then to Frankfurt. My mother was told that I was missing in action, and it was three months before she found out that I was a prisoner of war. I remained a POW for two years and three months. Near the end of the war, we were liberated by members of the 14th Armored Division (The Liberators) who had trained at Fort Campbell, Kentucky. I returned to my home in Kentucky on June 7, 1945.

I realize today that had the Germans not separated the Americans from the British before the escape, I would have very likely met the same fate of the 50 prisoners ordered shot by Adolf Hitler. Looking back at those difficult times during World War II, I know that I was equipped to deal with the ordeal as a POW. I grew up during the Depression, and the Christian heritage and faith instilled in me by family gave me the strength to survive.

Robert Waldrop
WWII • ETO

I would give the following advice to those in the military:

1. Stay in the best physical condition possible to be better prepared for any difficult assignments or hardships that you may encounter.

2. In the same manner, absorb the best training that is offered.

3. Continually practice self-discipline.

4. Communicate well with others so as to offer hope for survival and demonstrate a "never-give-up" attitude.

5. All of the above will be much easier to accomplish if you maintain your faith in God, your country, and your loved ones.

6. All of the above should be adhered to in everyday life, whether you are in the military or any other walk of life.

THAT WAS A GREAT DAY!

I was born in Fort Wayne, Indiana, on March 22, 1922. In 1942, after high school, I enlisted in the United States Army Air Corps. I attended and graduated from gunnery school in Nevada, following a number of different technical schools. I was finally assigned to a B-17 Bomber crew in October 1943. After completion of crew training in California and Tennessee, I headed to the European Theater of Operation and one of the many air bases in England. We were assigned to the 8th Air Force, 306th Bomb Group, and I was the crew's 1st armorer and a waist gunner.

We were shot down on our fifth mission, captured, and taken as prisoners of war on February 4, 1945. I was injured and had to spend several days in a German field hospital. When I was well enough, I was sent to the main interrogation center in Frankfurt. After the interrogations I was moved by train in a boxcar to Stalag Luft IV.

As the Russian Army advanced into Germany, we were force marched for three months during the middle of winter. Exhaustion and the bitter cold combined with an inadequate amount of food made for a miserable and even tenuous existence. How we survived with so little food and the freezing cold, only God knows. We were liberated in late April 1945. That was a great day!

Leonard Wallenmeyer
WWII • ETO

My advice for life is: Live a life that exhibits moral courage. Exodus 20:2-3 says "I am the Lord your God, who brought you out of Egypt, out of the land of slavery. You shall have no other gods before me." These verses contain the secret of a perfect relationship with God. God is supreme. Deep within the spirit of everyone is a longing to know a being greater than oneself. We Christians have a God who is great and good. He is our Father. Our God can step into any situation, no matter how impossible it appears, in order to bring us new hope and strength. How fortunate we are to know the living and loving God. The blessings that come from being in His presence are far greater than anyone can comprehend. In Him we find joy and purpose, hope, faith, forgiveness, and eternal life.

HE HAS BLESSED ME

I am 88 years old and have been blessed to have a living relationship with God for 75 years. I was raised on a farm by wonderful Christian parents. There were five children in the family, and I am the oldest. In 1941 I was drafted into the Army and was assigned to an infantry regiment. I felt very bad about this because I was being trained to kill people. I prayed about it and eventually I was assigned to a medical regiment; it was an answer to my prayer. Instead of killing people, I was trained to save lives. I believed, and still believe, it was the intervention of God in answer to prayer. I remained in that position until February 14, 1943, when I was captured by forces under the command of General Rommel and became a prisoner of war at the battle of Fiad Pass in Tunisia, North Africa. Prior to my capture, I took part in Operation Torch, the invasion of North Africa, beginning on November 8, 1942.

An entirely new life began for me when I became a prisoner of war. I was a POW for 800 days. It was by the grace of God that any of us survived this period of starvation, torture, and the ever-present possibility of being killed. Not knowing what the future might hold was always a great concern of every POW.

During the 800 days that I spent as a POW, God always seemed to protect me. I volunteered to work on a farm. As a non-commissioned officer, the Germans were not allowed, by the Geneva convention, to make us work. I believed that the physical labor would help to keep me healthy. I worked with 24 fellow POWs for 16 months doing farm work. We worked alongside 100 German workers, being kept in separate quarters. Working on the farm also allowed us more food than those who did not do farm work. The physical labor helped me to keep healthy in both body and spirit. During this time the Lord led me to be the chaplain of this group of 25 POWs, and every Sunday we were given the opportunity to feed our spiritual needs. This time was a definite blessing from our Lord.

On April 21, 1945, we were liberated by our allies, the Russians, and were told to remain in the POW camp. Some decided to leave, but many more remained until the end of the war. On May 8, 1945, American troops entered the camp, and we realized that we were finally on our way home to the United States. In France we were evaluated, received medical examinations, and processed for our return to the US. I received my final processing at Jefferson Barracks and was given a 60-day furlough to be followed by my discharge.

During my furlough, I married the girl that God made for me (she had waited all those years while I was in Europe). We raised a family and this summer we will celebrate our 60th wedding anniversary. I will be the first to acknowledge that as I look back on the events of my life, I see the hand of God in every circumstance. I have been blessed with good health and allowed to work at a number of jobs that I enjoyed. I have also had the good fortune to teach a Bible class for 60 years. He has blessed me to live for His purpose.

Colonel Edgar Whitcomb
U.S. Air Force (Ret.) • WWII • PTO

Success is earned, not necessarily crafted. It is attainable by all persons of all means and backgrounds. The hallmark for success is quite basic: to be in service to the Lord and to use the gifts He has entrusted to each of us for that purpose. How this is accomplished, though, is of utmost importance. The values of honesty, integrity, work ethic, and the compassion of "Do unto others..." mark the way we approach and accomplish life's work. How well we combine these determines personal success. How well this is accomplished in the eyes of the Lord determines significance.

THE LIGHT

I guess all ex-POWs have a story to share; mine is different than most. After I completed my training as a navigator, I was assigned to the Philippines at Clark Field. Following the attack on Pearl Harbor, the Japanese attacked the Philippines. I was able to escape from the mainland to the island of Corregidor but was captured by the Japanese. It was during this captivity that I met a young Marine officer named Bill, and we planned an escape from Corregidor, hoping to eventually get to China and home.

On May 22, 1942, at about two o'clock in the afternoon, we left the POW camp with a work detail of about 60 men to gather wood for the fires back in the camp. While going through the pretense of gathering wood, we wandered far to the north of the group which had scattered in the search for firewood. The guard was paying little attention to us. We found an old foxhole and jumped in. We frequently looked out over the edge of the hole but saw no one looking for us. After a long time, the sun began to sink behind the western hills, but it seemed like hours before darkness came.

As the darkness surrounded us, we headed to the edge of the water and at about 8:30 we lowered ourselves into the water to begin swimming. It seemed odd that only six weeks earlier we had made our way across the small channel in a boat fleeing Bataan. It was only two or three miles across from Corregidor back to Bataan at the closest point, and we believed it would be possible to swim the distance in a few hours. After about half an hour, we appeared to be a considerable distance from the shore; however, the dark outline of the Bataan coast seemed as far away as ever. Off in the distance we could see a light, and we decided to swim toward it so we could stay on course.

After awhile it began to sprinkle, and the water was no longer smooth. As we continued to swim, a large black cloud came across the sky. As the rain began to fall harder and the waves increased in size, I realized that I had not been in contact with Bill for a long time. I looked all about me, only to realize that the waves were so high that it was impossible to see in any direction.

"Hey, Bill!" I screamed as loud as I could. There was no answer. Again, I screamed, "Hey, Bill! Where are you?" I shouted again and again as I looked all about. The wind was blowing, the rain was coming down in torrents, and the waves were breaking over my head. The terrible thought struck me that something had happened to Bill. He was lost, and I was alone in the in the middle of the north channel. I continued to tread water and shout for Bill, but I was convinced that he would never answer.

It was then that I realized for the first time what a foolish idea this swim had been, and I understood why others back in the camp had ridiculed the idea of swimming to the mainland to escape. The reason that we had decided to try and escape is because we were sure that we would die if we remained in the prison camp. Again, I yelled, "Bill, where are you?" At the same time I realized that I was making no progress, although I was trying hard, but all I was able to do was bob like a cork in the big waves. Then I heard, "Ed!" I thought I saw a dark figure ahead and responded, "Bill, let's don't get lost again!'

He then said, "I wonder where we are? I haven't seen the light for a long time." "Neither have I," I answered. As we talked, we continued bobbing up and down with one big wave and then another. There was no use trying to swim; we were not able to make any headway, and we didn't have the slightest idea where we were and in which direction we needed to proceed. By this time we had been in the water at least three or four hours, and we should have been able to see the Bataan coast, but the sky was black, and the sea was black. There was nothing to do but to tread water until the storm subsided. It was a long time before the storm began to slacken. Finally it stopped completely, and we were able to see a tiny light shining in the distance. It took almost eight hours to reach the Bataan coast and what we thought was freedom.

Humanly, we all need to set goals, to set a course, and to remain on course. Life's inevitable storms will come, and all may seem lost, but continue to have faith and never lose hope. The same is true spiritually: set your course on the Light, have faith, and never lose hope no matter the spiritual storms that overtake you.

USS PUEBLO

The USS Pueblo was a U.S. Navy vessel sent on an intelligence mission off the coast of North Korea. On January 23, 1968, the USS Pueblo was attacked by North Korean naval vessels and MIG jets. One sailor was killed and several were wounded. The 82 surviving crew members were captured and held prisoner for 11 months.

THE HANOI HILTON

The French built the prison near the turn of the century with construction completed in 1901. The name, *Hoa Lo*, means "portable earthen stove." In the 19th century, families lived on the land where the prison was later built. They manufactured earthenware hibachis, called "hoa-lo." Streets became known by the name of the primary industry or commerce conducted on the street. After the French built the prison, they renamed the street "Rue de la Prison" or in Vietnamese, "Pho Nha Tu." When the French left, the Vietnamese changed the name of the street back to "Pho Hoa Lo" and the name of the prison to "Hoa Lo."

PANMUNJON TRUCE TALKS

Following agreement at the truce talks at Panmunjon, Operation Little Switch occurred April 20 – May 3, 1953. This was the exchange of sick and wounded prisoners of the Korean War. This was followed by Operation Big Switch on August 5 – December 23, 1953, the final exchange of prisoners of war by both sides.

John Wilcox
WWII • ETO

My advice for life is: One day at a time! At almost 85 years of age, each morning is a victory! It's the story of life, and we are stuck with it. Live one day at a time. Don't try to get ahead of God.

EACH MORNING, A VICTORY

I was inducted into the Army on October 3, 1941, and took my Basic Training at Camp Croft, South Carolina. I was assigned to the new command and the 805th Tank Destroyer Battalion at Fort Meade, Maryland. We were first shipped to England in August of 1942 and then to North Africa. We arrived in time to participate in the Tunisian campaign. During the battle of the Kasserine Pass, I was captured by Panzer troops of Field Marshal Rommel on February 17, 1943. I was taken to Tunis, then flown out by Junker 52s to Naples, Italy (my very first plane ride). From there we were moved by train, in boxcars, over the Alps to Germany. Thus began my two years and two months of captivity as a prisoner of war. We were liberated by the Russians and flown to England (my second plane ride). I was drafted on October 3, 1941, and discharged October 3, 1945.

The day of my capture, I was placed in an Arab hut with several other POWs. Rumors started that when the men were moved two at a time from the hut, they were to be executed. Wow! Prayer time began and continues to this day. Faith became my anchor. Luckily the rumors of executions were false.

In Stalag IIIB in Germany, we were able to build a chapel to be used by all denominations. I still have pen and ink drawings of the chapel and a list of the masses and novenas said for my family and friends. We had a Polish priest who conducted the services. I managed to get my POW log book home, which I worked on for over a year during my captivity.

To this day I continue to pray, "Thank you!" each evening before going to sleep. God has been good to me, providing me with the bread of life. I have ten grandchildren plus two great-grandchildren. My wonderful wife, Peg, passed away on March 3, 1989. We were wed on Valentine's Day, 1946. I carry on alone, taking each morning as a victory. I will soon be 85 years old—God willing!

Steven Woelk
USS Pueblo • North Korea

My Dad told me just prior to my going into the service, "You are who you run with." I was fortunate enough to have friends who were level-headed, honest, fun-loving, and willing to do anything for you when there was a need. I know my father was satisfied with the way I lived my life. I have tried to pass the same advice to my son as well. I would also offer this advice: No matter where you are or what you are facing, God is there and He is listening. No one, absolutely no one, anytime, anywhere in this world, can take the power of faith away from you.

OUR PRAYERS WERE ANSWERED

I was a young 19-year-old boy from Kansas when North Korea pirated the USS Pueblo off the high seas. I was critically wounded by shrapnel during the seizure of the Pueblo. Ten days after my capture, I was tied to a table and operated on with no anesthesia. Two weeks into my captivity, I was taken to a so-called North Korean hospital. It was actually a dirty, bedbug-infested building that we would classify as a warehouse in the United States. I spent the next 44 days in solitary confinement, clueless of what was happening elsewhere. I found out later that the crew was going through hell from severe beatings and long interrogations.

Unable to move and confined to a bed, I would watch the moon and the stars out the partially painted window above my bed. I hoped my mother was doing the same, since this was the only thing that we would have in common. (Later after I was released, she mentioned to me that she often looked at the moon and stars and would think of me.)

I did not attend church very often when I was growing up, but I did go to summer Bible school and church camp when I was 12 years old. At church camp we were required to get off by ourselves, meditate, and think about God. I remember sitting with my back against a large tree thinking that it was time to get serious about my faith and a belief in God. I made a vow on that hot, sultry summer day that I would start praying every day. I have kept that vow by thanking God for forgiving me for my sins and asking for His help during tough times. Korea was one of those tough times in my life.

We all believed that we would get out of the hellhole eventually, but we did not know how or when. God helped us all during that time, making us stronger to resist and to endure what was happening. It seemed that when one of us was having a lousy day, others would be up emotionally and in a good mood. We depended on each other every day. Our prayers were answered on December 23, 1968, when we were released and returned home to our families. The memories of 1968 will last for a lifetime.

I experienced other trials, but God helped me through those also. I went through a divorce but was later married again to the most wonderful person in my life. We had a child who was diagnosed with cancer at the age of six. We prayed for a miracle, but it was not to happen. Our daughter died nine months after the initial diagnosis. We were devastated, and our faith was tested to a great degree. We would not have been able to cope without God's help. Our daughter was a true gift from God, a true angel in every way. We made it through the sadness and loss, but it was not easy.

Later I would lose my mother, brother, and father within a three-year period. Part of my world fell apart when my father took his own life. Although my immediate family is gone now, I still have faith and dear memories of my loved ones. I do not know how I could have dealt with what happened to me without a faith in God. He continues to heal my pain. It does not come quickly, but it does come. One day it will be easier, and I will be reunited with my loved ones. God has blessed me all throughout my life. One just needs to let Him in.

Jack Woodson
WWII • PTO

Live life in such a way that your association with people, with God, and with our nation will be remembered with satisfaction. Strive to live a life with no regrets!

WELCOME HOME

My training as an ROTC cadet at the University of Oklahoma culminated in my being commissioned as a 2nd Lieutenant in the reserves. In April 1941, I was called to active duty and went to Fort Knox, Kentucky. I was then stationed at Fort Stotsenburg in the Philippines with the 17th Ordinance Company, a tank maintenance unit. All the training that I had previously received was only about winning battles. There was never a peep about losing them. We had heard about the code of conduct for those who were captured... "name, rank and service number" dictated by the Geneva convention.

We surrendered in April 1942 to the Japanese, but we were not prepared for the bestial treatment of the Bataan Death March. In January, prior to the surrender, we were put on half rations and then in April, quarter rations. Needless to say we were not in good shape. Many were suffering from malaria and/or dysentery. Those who were too sick to walk were killed by bullet, bayonet, or beating. I can close my eyes and still see those bodies every few yards along the road.

I had a small New Testament, which was an inspiration during my sojourn in Camp O'Donnell and at Cabanatuan. In September 1943, I was moved to Japan where I remained until the end of the war. In II Timothy 1:7 we read, "For God hath not given us the spirit of fear; but of power and of love, and of a sound mind" and in II Timothy 2:3 we read, "Thou therefore endure hardness as a good soldier of Jesus Christ." I also found great comfort in the Scriptures of Romans 8:28, "And we know that in all things God works for the good of those who love him, who have been called according to his purpose." And in II Corinthians 4:8-9, "We are hard pressed on every side, but not crushed; perplexed, but not in despair; persecuted, but not destroyed."

After the truce in August, our Air Force dropped food using red, white, and blue nylon parachutes. Some of the fellows made the four flags that represented the four nationalities of the men in the camp. What a sight to see the U.S., English, Dutch, and Norwegian flags rise to the top of the flagpoles. All we had seen for three and a half years was the flag with the rising sun. If a flag burner would have appeared at that ceremony, he would not have survived!

We traveled back to the United States on a troop ship which was scheduled to arrive in San Francisco in the early morning. Everyone gathered along the rail of the ship shortly after daybreak hoping to see the Golden Gate Bridge. What a disappointment when we were met with dense fog—we couldn't see 50 feet ahead! Our spirits began to sink, but suddenly the fog seemed to part. Both ends of the bridge were still encased in the fog, but the center section was bathed in bright sunlight—what a welcome! I don't believe there was a dry eye in the entire bunch. We were home! We could see our families and friends who had agonized about us during our captivity standing along the pier. What a welcome...God bless America!

Eugene Wopata
WWII • ETO

Hard work never hurt anyone; in fact, working hard to achieve your goals is the key that opens the lock to human success. Always be honest, and do what you know is right. The spiritual advice that I would offer is this: Put your trust in God and live by the Golden Rule.

FREEDOM IS NOT FREE

I grew up in a rural community in southwest Nebraska, the only child of a typical Midwestern family in the Depression era. I was inducted into the Army in 1944 and completed basic training in Texas that summer. The 42nd Rainbow Division arrived in southern France in December 1944 and was involved in the Battle of the Bulge.

I believe the Lord was watching over me because we experienced a great deal of artillery shelling and also small arms fire. When I was captured by the German Army, a German soldier demonstrated compassion for me, a wounded enemy soldier, and spared my life.

During the long days of captivity that I experienced in Stalag IVB, God gave me the hope and courage to endure starvation and loneliness. The Russians liberated our camp on April 23, 1945. A short time later, an American jeep entered the prison camp, flying the American flag.

This was a truly awesome sight. To me, the flag is a reminder of the freedom that I enjoy today. Many gave some, but others gave all, in order for me to enjoy this freedom. Freedom is not free!

About the Author...

COLONEL JIM COY served as a medical consultant for the U.S. Army Special Operations Command. He served two years as the national president of the Special Operations Medical Association and as the national surgeon of the Reserve Officers Association. He lectures nationally and internationally on combat trauma medicine and about his research using lightweight x-ray equipment. He has served with numerous Special Operations units and served with the 3rd Group, Army Special Forces (Airborne) in the 1991 Gulf War.

His military awards, badges, and honors include the Legion of Merit, the Defense Meritorious Service Medal, the Combat Medic Badge, Expert Field Medic Badge, Flight Surgeon Badge, Airborne, Air Assault, and Israeli Airborne Badges. He has also received the Order of Military Merit from the Army Medical Regiment and the prestigious "A" designation—the highest recognition of the Army Medical Department. From 1978-1989 he battled with cancer and had four major surgeries during which portions of his tongue, throat, and jawbone were removed. Today he is considered cured.

Jim and his wife, Vicki, have three children: Tim, Tricia, and Joshua. His family is extremely important to him. He has a vision for men becoming spiritual leaders and standing strong for their families. Colonel Coy is active in Promise Keepers and Men Without Fear, a local interdenominational group for men, and he is the Men's Ministry director in his home church. Today, Jim desires to develop a ministry to military and former military men and frequently speaks to community, church, and military groups across the nation. Colonel Coy is the author of the Eagles series books that include: *A Gathering of Eagles, 2nd Ed.*, and *Valor: A Gathering of Eagles*. Currently he is working on other books in the series to include, *Those Who Serve*, and *Servants, Shepherds and Saints*. The profit from the book series is used for scholarships to send kids with financial needs to Christian and parochial schools.

MEN WITHOUT FEAR—777

During the Persian Gulf War, I served with the 3rd Group Army Special Forces, (Airborne). In preparation for the ground war, and as one of the soldiers selected to go forward with the invasion into Kuwait City, I was required to meet with members of our military intelligence section. The purpose of this meeting was to discuss the possibility of capture and of being an Iraqi POW. We were asked a myriad of questions for possible use by those who would be involved in a rescue attempt. One scenario was a rescue attempt after many years as an Iraqi POW. During this extensive interview, our responses to the various questions were written down and recorded and would be used to ensure our correct identification by those who would attempt to rescue us. I remember one question vividly because of my answer. The question was, "What number or series of numbers would you give to those who, during a rescue attempt, would ask for your numerical code number?" We were instructed not to use birthdays, anniversaries, phone numbers, or ID numbers because the enemy might have access to them. I decided on the number 777. My reasoning was spiritual. Many Bible scholars believe the number 7 to be an important number because of its use in the Bible. I felt the number 777 would be easy to remember because I would remember the number 7 for God the Father, the next 7 as God the Son, and the last 7 as God the Holy Spirit.

BIBLICAL REFERENCE

With my return home from the Gulf, my faith, already strong, continued to increase. I began to make a conscious effort to seek God daily and made a decision to live a life dedicated to Him. During one of my daily times of Bible study, I remembered my 777 answer. I began to search the Bible for the number 777. The only mention of the number 777 was that Noah's father lived to be 777 years old. Still searching, I decided to look in the seventh book of the Bible, the seventh chapter, and the seventh verse. I turned to Judges, the 7th book of the Bible, to the 7th chapter, and read the 7th verse: "And the Lord said unto Gideon, By the three hundred men that lapped will I save you and deliver the Midianites into thine hand: and let the other people go every man unto his place." As I began to read and re-read this story about Gideon, I realized a truth in the passage that is relevant even today. Let me quickly review the story with you. Verse 2 reads, "The Lord said the people are too many, lest Israel will say my own hand hath saved me." In verse 3, God told Gideon to "proclaim whoever is fearful let him return." Twenty-two thousand returned; only ten thousand remained. I concluded that two-thirds of the men were fearful. This meant that only one-third were MEN WITHOUT FEAR.

In verse 4, the Lord said, "The people are yet too many. Bring them down to the water." There were 10,000 men without fear, but God would use only 300 men. In verse 5, the Lord said, "Everyone that lappeth of the water set by himself; likewise everyone that boweth down to drink." Verse 6 tells us about the 300 hundred men who, while standing, lapped water with their hand to their mouth, and the rest bowed down. Although 9,700 men were MEN WITHOUT FEAR, they bowed down to drink. Only 300 remained erect, drinking water from their hand. In my opinion these men who remained upright were looking for the enemy. They were PREPARED for battle. In verse 7, the Lord said, "By the 300 men will I save you." The number 300 is less than one percent of the original 32,000 soldiers.

As I studied and re-studied this passage, I tried to understand its relevance for today. I came to the conclusion that even today, God continues to use only a small number of men. He uses a similar plan, a similar equation, spiritually speaking. In my experience, about one-third of men seem to be MEN WITHOUT FEAR—men seeking to serve God. These are men and women who have decided to follow God. God, however, will only use a very small number of people to fulfill His divine plan.

HOW CAN I BE USED BY GOD?

How does God determine and then select these individuals? God uses only a few men to fulfill His divine plan. He does not intend for man to receive the glory for His plan or for what He is doing. I believe that God separates His people by selecting those who are WITHOUT FEAR, those WILLING to be used, those SEEKING to be used, those who have PREPARED themselves to be used by God, and most importantly, those WILLING TO GIVE GOD THE GLORY for the victory.

You might ask the question, "How can I become one of the few who are really used by God to fulfill His divine plan?" I am convinced that first, you have to be in the Word every day. Second, you have to be in prayer every day, and third, you must frequently meet with others of like heart, mind, soul, and purpose. This will help you to be prepared to be used by God! Finally you must be willing to give God the glory for what He is doing, what He has done, and what He is going to do!

—Colonel Jim Coy (Ret.)

To contact the author:
COL Jim Coy
www.agatheringofeagles.com
coyjv@socket.net

To contact Family Net to obtain the Prisoners of Hope video:

Family Net Products
6350 West Freeway
Fort Worth, TX 76116

800-777-1127

Other books by Colonel Jim Coy

A Gathering of Eagles–2nd Ed.
Three hundred forty-five Medal of Honor recipients, ex-POWs, and leaders in the military, political, and religious arenas share their core beliefs about leadership and success. It demonstrates what makes America great. Photos included of each one.

Among the leaders featured are: Rear Adm. Jeremiah Denton (Ret.), J.C. Watts, Jr., Colin Powell, Billy Graham, James Dobson, Chuck Swindoll, Larry Burkett, Roger Staubach, Gary Smalley, Joseph Stowell, and many more.
ISBN 1-58169-049-5 304 pg. 6 x 9 $14.99

VALOR: A Gathering of Eagles
A book about courage and faith from 117 Medal of Honor recipients. Includes their photos and official Medal of Honor citations describing how they made courageous breakthroughs under combat conditions. The men also share how their core beliefs and faith in God sustained them through various combat crises and beyond military life.
ISBN 1-58169-111-4 320 pg. 5.5 x 8.5 PB $14.99

EX-POW RESOURCES

WEB PAGE ADDRESSES

www.axpow.org
www.nampows.org
www.pownetwork.org
www.pow-foundation.org
www.pow-miafamilies.org

BOOKS BY CO-AUTHORS

UNCHAINED EAGLE — Robert Certain

TWO SOULS INDIVISIBLE — (Jim Hirsch) Fred Cherry, Porter Halyburton

BEYOND SURVIVAL — Jerry Coffee

RETURN WITH HONOR — George Day

WHEN HELL WAS IN SESSION — Jeremiah Denton

FAITH BEYOND BELIEF — David Eberly

STAYING ALIVE — Carl Fyler

CAPTIVE WARRIOR: A VIETNAM POWs STORY — Sam Johnson

A LONG WALK HOME — Clarence Larson

FAITH OF MY FATHERS — John McCain

SCARS AND STRIPES — Eugene McDaniel

YET ANOTHER VOICE — Norm McDaniel

THE HANOI COMMITMENT — James Mulligan

I'M NO HERO and THE LAST DOMINO — Charlie Plumb

FROM NORTH AFRICA TO NAZI PRISON CAMPS — Murray Pritchard

LOVE AND DUTY — Ben Purcell

THE PASSING OF THE NIGHT — Robinson Risner

COURAGE UNDER FIRE and **IN LOVE & WAR** — James & Sybil Stockdale

ESCAPE FROM CORREGIDOR — Edgar Whitcomb